# PRAISE FO
# THE WICKED (

"It's a wicked world, and we live in wicked times, facing complex challenges that are intractable (and even incomprehensible) to traditional, tame—that is to say mechanistic and reductionistic—tools, organizations, strategies, and mindsets. Marcus Kirsch wades right in to wrassle the beast to the ground. Get in there and get dirty with him."

**—GIL PHILIP FRIEND**, CEO NATURAL LOGIC, INC. CEO, CRITICAL PATH CAPITAL. FORMER CHIEF SUSTAINABILITY OFFICER, CITY OF PALO ALTO

"For those who believe in a people-first and design led approach to change, this book is a must read—let the Wicked games begin!"

**—RACHEL HIGHAM**, MANAGING DIRECTOR, BT IT

"If knowing the problem is half of the solution, then *The Wicked Company* is a vital piece to understanding the challlenges ahead for any organisation."

**—ROBERT ROWLAND SMITH**, AUTHOR *THE REALITY TEST*, FOUNDER-DYNAMICS OF POWER

"The essential follow up to *The Innovator's Dilemma*, *The Wicked Company* makes real 'The New Normal'—the world where the problem we are working on is changing faster than we can solve it, so we are swapping out engines on the airplane that is still in flight. *The Wicked Company* makes the case that the only way to succeed in this environment is to radically restructure your company's processes to not just handle change, but to ride the wave of progress into success and profitability."

**—GREG NUDELMANN**, DIRECTOR OF UX, DESIGN CAFFEINE INC.

*The Wicked Company*

by Marcus Kirsch

ISBN 978-1-63393-973-8

Published by

 köehlerbooks™

210 60th Street
Virginia Beach, VA 23451
800–435–4811
www.koehlerbooks.com

WHEN GROWTH IS NOT ENOUGH.

# THE WICKED COMPANY

## MARCUS KIRSCH

VIRGINIA BEACH
CAPE CHARLES

To my Pommie. May the wickedness of the universe be inspiring and exciting to you instead of challenging and overwhelming, and may the stars shine bright for you every night.

Thanks to my mother, Carolina, Troy, Tom, Graham, Sheldon, Rob, Marc, Ali, Ms. Dowdle, and all the others who were patient enough to listen to my ramblings before they started to make sense.

Some crowdfunding thanks to Andres Monsalve, Brigitte Lyding, Daniel Hirschmann, David Gardner, Jean Tiquet, Michael Antonio, Neal Schaffer, Robert Frith and Steve May.

# TABLE OF CONTENTS

FOREWORD BY TROY NORCROSS . . . . . . . . . . . . . . . . . X
WHY WRITE THIS BOOK? . . . . . . . . . . . . . . . . . . 1
THE FROG IN THE BOILING WATER . . . . . . . . . . . . . . 3

**PART I: DON'T LOOK BACK IN ANGER** . . . . . . . . . . . .7
DEATH OF A TRAVELING CRAFTSWOMAN . . . . . . . . . . .9
YOU HAVE BEEN DESKILLED! . . . . . . . . . . . . . . . .16
JUST ADD SILO! . . . . . . . . . . . . . . . . . . . . . 23
ZERO FRICTION . . . . . . . . . . . . . . . . . . . . . 32

**PART II: OOPS, I DID IT AGAIN!** . . . . . . . . . . . . . . 37
THE MINDSET-TOOL-WORLD FEEDBACK LOOP . . . . . . . . 39
OBJECT-ORIENTED PROGRAMMING:
YOUR BRAIN IN 1,000 NUTSHELLS . . . . . . . . . . . . . 49
SEAN PARKER IS THE DEVIL . . . . . . . . . . . . . . . . 60
PIRATE BAY, THE MOST AWESOME CANCER . . . . . . . . . 64
POPCORN TIME . . . . . . . . . . . . . . . . . . . . . 68
ILLEGAL! THIS TIME: BITCOIN . . . . . . . . . . . . . . . .71
DON'T GET ME STARTUPPED . . . . . . . . . . . . . . . . 84
WICKED IS HERE . . . . . . . . . . . . . . . . . . . . . 89

**PART III: WICKED GAMES** . . . . . . . . . . . . . . . . . . **93**

WHAT NOT TO DO . . . . . . . . . . . . . . . 96

THE TWO TYPES OF SMART . . . . . . . . . . . . . .105

THE 1,000 FACES OF INNOVATION . . . . . . . . . . 121

TOWER OF BABEL . . . . . . . . . . . . . . .133

VALUE CHANGE: TAME TO WICKED . . . . . . . . . . .140

FIGHTING A SILVERBACK GORILLA . . . . . . . . . . .147

GOVERNMENT IS NEXT . . . . . . . . . . . . . . . .155

MARKET WITHOUT A NAME . . . . . . . . . . . . . . .157


EPILOGUE . . . . . . . . . . . . . . . . . . .160

ABOUT THE AUTHOR . . . . . . . . . . . . . . . . .164

# FOREWORD
# BY TROY NOCROSS

PROBLEMS. THEY SAY THE best entrepreneurs have a deep understanding of the problem they are trying to solve. Moreover, the best companies can reliably and efficiently solve a specific type of problem over and over again. However, there are some problems—wicked problems—which require new thinking and approach. They need a shift in the strategy, the organisation and the people.

The ivory tower of design thinking is one to be torn down in this new paradigm. To solve today's problems, everyone in the organisation can and should apply wicked problems solving skills and design thinking is only one of them. Successful companies of tomorrow will be wicked companies—with cross-disciplinary teams and processes in place to help them solve wicked problems.

Marcus Kirsch is uniquely positioned to lead the charge for this transformational shift in problem-solving. He has the degree of a design practitioner, the eye and hand of an artist and designer and the sharp and challenging wit of a savant. Marcus also has an affable personality to make the entire conversation of change a friendly ongoing debate. He has worked in large multi-national corporations and built startup funding projects spanning countries and continents. Most importantly, Marcus has had years of experience spotting wicked problems and building and running teams to find wicked solutions.

I've known Marcus for over four years. We have spent hours discussing and debating problems ranging from user experiences for banking apps through to how to explain blockchain without using words. There are energy and a passion in our discussions as we bounce off each other and challenge each other and force ourselves to look at situations through ever-evolving lenses. Whenever possible, we add new people to the mix. They always come with eclectic skillsets and experiences. Anyone can join, and everyone brings their design thinking skills—even if they may not call it that. We tend to look at them as modern polymaths.

For my sins, I started my career on 4,000 acres of farmland before leaping into the software world of flight-simulators. I've been in tech fields ranging from telecoms to consumer data and winding up in blockchain. I have seen many problems over the years. Now that I have the right language, I know that they were wicked problems. Now I know they require a different approach and different teams to be able to solve.

Over the years, I watched companies fail to solve these problems because they were stuck applying the same old approach to a different type of problem. I watched others succeed in spades for reasons, to the casual observer, which may have looked like a blend of luck and brute force. *The Wicked Company* will show you there was a lot more going on that just wasn't visible and how you can apply it too.

If you are looking for insight, guidance and truly actionable suggestions on how to spot and deal with the most wicked (and the most profitable) problems, *The Wicked Company* is the book. This is the book that's going to sit on the corner of your desk. Or it's the one you'll hide in your backpack to give you a strategic edge over the rest of the competition.

*The Wicked Company* will help you join the movement bringing a new organisational mindset to address today's wicked problems.

**—Troy Norcross,**
ORACLE—
Blockchain Practice Lead EMENA

# WHY WRITE THIS BOOK?

We become what we behold. We shape our tools and
then our tools shape us.

−Father John Culkin (not Marshal McLuhan)

We shape our tools the way we describe reality.
When the tools shape us, they describe the way we are
allowed to describe reality.

−That guy who wrote this book

Edgar Allan Poe describes *disentanglement* as the ambition of the
mind to make sense of the world. Understanding the world is
mastering it, and we all know how flawed a goal this can be. We
can never know everything, and all we have are different tools that
allow us to reflect on various data, different paradigms that help us
make sense of it.

Jacques Derrida, the father of deconstructivism, describes his
approach as to look at two opposites and being able to see the space
in between. Disentangling previously polarised notions and filling
them with new understanding and insights has become a new
opportunity for successful companies.

This is the era of wicked companies. Why wicked? Because we live
in a world of wicked problems, problems that are very complex and

1

change their requirements while we are working on their solutions. Wicked companies have teams and people who are more like polymaths than specialists and who combine an eclectic mix of capabilities and expertise. A wicked company has its opposite in the traditional. tame company that has existed since the Industrial Revolution.

Everyone can create a wicked company, but to do so, a new mindset around capabilities, governance, teams, and the support for the outcomes is needed. If you ever ask yourself why your company is struggling to do better in today's world, you are probably using tame company aspects to solve wicked problems.

I never wanted to write a book, but some ideas are so stubborn that they keep popping up. Through positive feedback from friends, peers, and evidence from projects, they eventually snowball into manifestation. The narrative of the wicked company designed to solve wicked problems best describes the needs and business phenomena I have been observing for nearly twenty years. I knew I wanted to get this idea out there to everyone who wants to know more. I hope it will help you understand today's world a bit more easily.

I hope you support and enjoy my book.

**Marcus Kirsch**

# THE FROG IN THE BOILING WATER

The most exciting breakthroughs of the twenty-first century will not occur because of technology, but because of an expanding concept of what it means to be human.

–John Naisbitt

Paradigm shifts don't just happen overnight. They evolve and grow gradually, often unseen by many. When they have the right maturity, they will come out in the open, having developed the correct narrative to spread across the world.

There is a fable[1] of a frog sitting in a pot of water slowly increasing in temperature. The frog does not realize this until it is too late and he is killed in the boiling water. This is where some industries are today. The next paradigm shift has been sneaking up on them.

We assume things are changing so fast that no one can keep up with the pace. We believe the next technology will bring another gold rush, another market, and even higher evaluations and prosperity for everyone.

I do not believe this to be true.

The characteristics and behaviors of what is surrounding us have changed. This change requires a new mindset to make us more familiar and at ease with the new characteristics. The reason why things feel overwhelming and uncomfortable is that what is around us does not do what we expect it to do. It feels unpredictable, fast, and cryptic, like only specialists and gurus can make sense of it. This is not the case.

I believe one only needs to see the difference between understanding what a tame problem is, what a wicked problem is, and how to look at and approach this new set of behaviors. Once you see all this, you will be part of the new mindset, things will slow down, and the next trend won't feel as new or overwhelming. This is how it worked for me in the last twenty years, and I will be trying my best with this book so that it does the same for you.

Before I start with the long story, I want to define a few terminologies that I will be using throughout the book.

**TAME PROBLEM[2]:** A problem that does not change while you are working on it. Building a bridge is a tame problem. You can measure where to build the bridge, and the terrain will not change while you are creating it. Mass production is considered a tame problem. Tame problems are solved by companies designed to solve those kinds of problems well—tame companies, if you will.

**WICKED PROBLEM[2]:** A problem that changes after you started working on it. Creating a service like Uber is such a problem. The people who use the service will behave differently once they get used to it. It will perform differently if there are more or fewer cars or more or fewer users. Having a competing service can change price expectations, et cetera.

The service economy started many decades ago. Today we have begun to design services. In 1999, Starbucks was one of the first companies named as being part of the experience economy, which changed the quality and complexity level of what consumers expect and use. These and whatever comes next are wicked problems. Wicked problems are solved by companies designed to address those kinds of problems well. Wicked companies, if you will.

**MINDSET:** The thing you use to describe the world; your inner model to explain why things are the way they are and what therefore is considered a sensible or good solution to a problem. An excellent example of what a mindset can do is the famous saying, "If all you have is a hammer, everything looks like a nail."

**TOOLS:** The things we use to create stuff, from hammers to software, hardware devices, and network services like the internet or our trains. All of those contribute to what we can imagine creating and how we can create it.

**WORLD:** Our current reality, especially the people in it and the expectations, needs, and behaviors they represent.

So how do we get to understand the new aspects needed to create a wicked company?

We will first have a look at the characteristics of tame problems and mindsets of tame companies by looking at the Industrial Revolution, a time that redefined how we work and what we create. We will then look at the new technologies brought to us to understand what the new wicked problems are made of and why. I will be making the case that most of what we consider new is just the same thing in different colors, incrementally improved to fit the next industry. In the last part, we will look at what a wicked company needs in order to deal with wicked problems.

And I will not use the word "digital" a single time to do so.

# PART I

# DON'T LOOK BACK IN ANGER

**Knowing the problem is half of the solution.
Let's start tame.**

Change is not merely necessary to life; it is life.

—Alvin Toffler, 1970

# DEATH OF A TRAVELING CRAFTSWOMAN

Imagine Leonardo da Vinci trying to find a job during the Industrial Revolution. Today, he would probably own a startup or change his name to Elon Musk.

During the Industrial Revolution, we turned craftsmen and women into single-skilled workers. It was an appropriate solution to the tame problem of mass production. We lost the concept of constant learning and the idea of mastery and gained, at the time, our perceived path to a better life. Simplify people's contributions to the work environment to mass produce identical products in the absence of appropriate machines.

Today, we have robots and automation that make cheap mass production a commodity. Will people, therefore, lose their jobs or pick up more complex work as they did before their potential was minimized for a greater good?

Before the Industrial Revolution, that is how workers were described: as craftsmen and craftswomen. Skills or jobs were understood to be learned over an extended period, often a lifetime. Continuous learning was a default. Craftsmen would not only improve their skills, but build and iterate their tools. Combining the theoretical with the practical, they would improve their craft by exploring many aspects beyond their immediate context. Painters would build their canvases, go into nature to collect ingredients for different paints, and generally further their understanding of biology, chemistry, and manufacturing to improve their painting.

Artists—or craftsmen—like Leonardo da Vinci are undoubtedly exceptional, but his diversity proves how considering many skills and thinking models can improve the variety and impact of an outcome. It was natural for him to look outside the box for new knowledge and solutions.

Today's jobs don't resemble that approach. Modern companies don't require such diversity in a resource because they are not structured for diversity to come to fruition easily. Imagine Leonardo da Vinci working in a factory on a conveyor belt: a painter, a sculptor, a medical researcher, an engineer of bridges, and military equipment. Recruiters and employers would be confused about where to put him because skills are tightly controlled silos within departments and industries. It is all verticals, and verticals mean knowledge, which does not easily move.

Traditionally, companies are not looking for self-starters, which eliminates people with multiple skills and opinions beyond a single silo. There is a reason why Elon Musk is better off as an entrepreneur. He is arguably good at starting a company, but not to be hired by one. Leonardo da Vinci surely fits that pattern.

However, the value of single-skilled people has been depleting in recent years. Self-learners, cross-disciplinary workers, or horizontal teams are becoming increasingly important to solve business challenges and create new opportunities. Most transformation projects go through a round of identifying those characteristics in a workforce, to use them as early adopters of change. Startups consist of small teams with multiple and diverse responsibilities.

Service design, or design thinking, is an old design practice experiencing a profound renaissance. It is one of the most cross-disciplinary professions, combining research, design, prototyping, workshop facilitation, and people skills with production, operational design, and business modeling. Its essence is to bring people from a variety of backgrounds together to investigate a problem from different angles. This is what people mean when they talk about collaboration today: holistic observation and investigation of a problem to find the best possible solution.

Today a collaborative approach does not mean a group of people in a room, it means breaking down silos to get a more complete picture of the problem.

This is not a fad. Some of the more progressive educational institutions are recognizing that companies need a different workforce. The Massachusetts Institute of Technology has started asking for applicants with cross-disciplinary skill sets, identifying the benefits of horizontal rather than "siloed" skills.[3]

If you are looking at the world with this mindset, you might think that single-skill silos or specializations are running out of steam to find solutions for the future.

Tim Carmichael, Ex-CDO/CAO of the British Army, makes it evident that horizontal, collaborative thinking had indeed been identified by the military as the most effective way forward. If someone like the military considers a shift in approach, it is worth listening to.

I remember back in the '70s and '80s, my teachers told me that all I had to do in life was to learn one single thing I was good at and then do that until I retire. This single-skill career is not our reality anymore. We need a workforce that is closer to what craftsmen and craftswomen were: self-learning and ever evolving. We are losing a lot of value if we are taming people into single-skilled robots.

For a long time, businesses have been struggling to keep single-skill workers motivated and productive. There is boredom and frustration in being a small cog in a big wheel. Our brains are not made for it. To fight this boredom, people are sometimes told to take a hobby. The larger the company, the more likely it is to offer extra activities like football clubs and yoga classes. These aim to improve morale, purpose, and retention, but they often feel like a placebo for hobbies, a quick fix for the lack of diversity in someone's job. Does this not feel artificial, inefficient, or unnecessary?

Today, most people learn a new job in three months, and then it becomes repetitive and often underwhelming. But when guilds and craftsmen and craftswomen were still the dominant contributors to innovation, learning a skill required a lifetime because so many different pieces of knowledge had to be considered and evaluated. Back then, having a job could be as complex as life itself. Being a craftsman was a very intellectual endeavor, at times even requiring traveling across different cultures to gain more varied knowledge.

Carpenters still practice this approach today. The "Wanderjahre,"[4] or journeyman years, mean junior carpenters travel by foot to work on different projects across different regions, learning a diverse set of skills and viewpoints surrounding their craft. The equivalent of this is sending your workers to different companies to experience different variations of the same processes or learn new tools. This would then widen their horizons, and they would come back to apply the learnings in the best possible way. Which company does things like that today? Would it not be more sustainable to have people who iteratively learn, test, and improve things?

In some places, we can still see a focus on lifetime learning, too. Japanese arts like calligraphy, sword-making, or being a sushi chef are produced with a mindset that believes in years of insight and constant learning. Knowing everything there is to know about a given task is the essence of understanding and quality. It is expected to take a lifetime to achieve perfection in a craft.

Why are hobbies so separated from contributing to your job at work? As it turns out, many innovations come from people tinkering in their own time with ideas similar to what they do at work; yet they often fail to contribute or to gain recognition at work.

Google has recognized this problem and largely avoided it, at least in its early days. Two of its biggest inventions, Gmail and

AdWords, came from people tinkering outside of business as usual. The latter especially would become a large revenue stream for the company. This innovation did not come out of formal work; it came from a few workers doing things outside of their silos. There is a history of people leaving companies that did not recognize their interests and therefore lost significant value and potential. Is our classic business setup ignoring characteristics like self-learning and alternative activities on purpose?

The siloed structure of companies can create confusion when it collides with a person who has eclectic capabilities. My bachelor's degree was in graphic design. Around 1998, I learned how to code websites, then apps and hardware. In short, I was a designer who could code and a coder who could design. I won't even mention the art- and human-centered research capabilities I acquired around 2000.

In most of my interviews after my master's degree, when my experience covered at least three silos of capabilities, I experienced confusion. The companies were looking for a single, deskilled set of capabilities for tame problem-solving. For some reason, no one saw the extra value I could bring. This was twenty years ago.

The essence of the meeting went a bit like this:

"So, are you a coder or a designer?"

"Well, I am both."

Silence.

"We need to either put you into our development team or our design team."

"Don't you have an integrated process?"

"No, you have to be one or the other."

"No problem, which one do you need?"

"But you are neither."

"I think I am both; you get two for one."

"I don't know how that fits into our process."

The conversation ended somewhere with, "We need to think about what we can do with you."

Today, T-shaped[5] people that have secondary and tertiary skill sets are heavily sought after. A great team member means being anything from a researcher to a facilitator of workshops; an analyst to a maker of physical or code-based prototypes; a developer of business cases to an operational modeler. These are the people needed to be comfortable around wicked problems.

Craftsmen and women used to have cross-disciplinary tendencies, or you could say that their crafts integrated other views and skills. Their continuous learning would make them deconstruct existing solutions to build new and better ones. They moved between theory and practice freely. Doing so was part of their job. The term "outside the box" is essentially describing the ability to step outside one's silo or constraint. Today, this is hailed as a feature. Back then, it was part of everyday business. One of the most significant facts is that we shaped education toward creating silos, rather than enabling learning across disciplines.

## The only thing that interferes with my learning is education.

### —Albert Einstein

How much does our modern approach decrease the aggregate synergetic value and benefit of a complex human being? I am not the first to say education might need a revision. What we might want to consider is making constant learning a part of every job. Instead of making workers uncomfortable because learning phases are the exception, let's make it a continuous aspect of working life again.

A few weeks back, I surveyed LinkedIn to find out to what extent of people's skills are underused in their jobs. The overwhelming majority felt less than 50 percent of their skill set was being utilized at their workplace. What does that tell us?

Study the science of art. Study the art of science.
Develop your senses—especially learn how to see.
Realize that everything connects to everything else.

—Leonardo da Vinci

Outliers like Elon Musk and Leonardo da Vinci do not support the idea that everyone can be a polymath, but science has shown a correlation between having multiple skills and having success and impact.

As Robert Root-Bernstein notes in *Multiple Giftedness in Adults: The Case of Polymaths,*[6] "Creativity researchers often assert that specialization is a requirement for adult success, that skills and knowledge do not transfer across domains, and that the domain dependence of creativity makes general creativity impossible."

If either high specialization or cross-disciplinary disposition are giving us a statistical edge on being successful and solving the world's challenges, why are we only trying one of those approaches?

People are naturally diverse and multi-skilled. We have multiple skills at different levels because we are built to learn throughout our lifetime. The more we know, the more options we have. The more we embrace a multitude of views, the closer we are to deconstructive thinking. Life is a wicked problem and we are built to deal with it. This makes us designed to deal with wicked problems. Tame problems are artificial simplifications. The Industrial Revolution was an artificial way to restrict our potential to solve a tame problem. We need to recover from it. Our complex future needs this. You might argue that we are living in an era of wicked problems.

In the next chapter, we will be looking at the pivotal moment that reduced humans into single-skilled resources.

# YOU HAVE BEEN DESKILLED!

During the Industrial Revolution, many inventions helped make mass production viable. Before robots and modern communication tools, Henry Ford separated the theoretical aspect of a craft from production. Knowledge and learning would sit with management; execution of tasks would rest with the workers. He called this *deskilling*.[7] He turned people into robots and made mass production happen.

Few people are only good at one thing. Everyone comes with a diverse range of skills. Not all of them will get you a job, but all contribute to your way of looking at a problem. Sometimes, it is the combination of those different areas of knowledge that results in an intriguing blend of expertise. In a further chapter, I will give evidence of the combination of skills as a source of success called polymath. The Industrial Revolution stripped us of this; it separated execution from thinking.

In 1913, steam engines contributed to the early automation of factories. For most parts of the process, you still needed people. Trained workers were expensive. The question was how to create cheaper labor. Henry Ford was the inventor not of the conveyor belt but of large-workforce mass production. Ford's splitting of theory and practice and siloing of practical execution into separate tasks made it possible to hire low-skilled workers cheaply and by the thousands.

By definition, mass production is a tame problem. Any product produced is the same before the idea enters the factory and will be the same when it leaves the factory. It won't change afterward either: shipping and delivery time remain the same. This means current places of mass production and companies that clone each other's products are tame companies, companies that are good at solving tame problems. Their structure has evolved to become even more rigid and niche.

In *The Zero Marginal Cost Society,* Jeremy Rifkin[8] gives an elaborate record of some of the first significant modern corporate undertakings. Projects like the Pacific Railway created the need for large and complex communications across the U.S. It was a managerial nightmare for all companies involved.

When all they had was telegraphs and paper-based communication, changes and challenges had to be handled by people on location rather than being signed by company headquarters, or they had to be delayed, which was costly. As companies did not have modern communication channels, they needed to compensate with layers of management and communication personnel riding by horseback to communicate progress and actions across the project.

Three companies were incorporated to achieve the previously unthinkable. Matching rail tracks in the middle of a big continent was no small undertaking. These early days have shaped our understanding of corporate structures and processes more than anything. At the time, it was an astonishing achievement, and building 3,000 kilometers of railroad between four companies would not be easy even today. One might compare it to the building of the pyramids. It was an enormous project with the help of both private and governmental funding.

But once it was set up, people rode back and forth to communicate tasks and report updates from headquarters on each coast to production crews and between companies. This became a model other companies copied. The idea of management as a communication layer was a success.

Today, for the most part, we have live video and audio in the most remote places. Devices and networks have replaced managers and messengers, but not at the companies. In our private lives, we use an impressive arsenal of tools. Companies still have an army of managers and meetings full of people with responsibilities and reporting functions that no one needs anymore. This also leads to sign-off bottlenecks and unnecessary politics to maintain decision-makers who are just not needed anymore. Automation will only accelerate the inevitable.

Rifkin's account of the first large corporate undertakings is an example of companies trying to tackle more complex problems. The problems were still tame, not wicked—just bigger and more complex. Their requirements did not change over the time of creating a solution. The result of this was that more extensive and complex managerial layers separating thinking from execution. It split the why and the how within a company. In the absence of robots and mobile communication, one could only manage mass production at cost could only be achieved by redefining a worker's meaning and value.

Today's corporations can be much leaner if they enable their workers not just to do more, but to be more. Fewer people with broader skills can tackle issues in multiple ways; they now have the tools to find the alternative that fits the business best, without layers of managers who only act as communication and reporting proxies.

If you think about it, layers of managers inevitably create games of Chinese whispers and power politics. Just like every click in the purchase journey of Amazon reduces the rate of conversion, managers sitting between the source and the destination lose pieces of information that can be essential and add time—and therefore costs—to any project. The baseline of production has shifted.

Creating a product or even a working—not necessarily a good—service is a commodity.

Ken Robinson stated in his TED Talk[9] that there is evidence schools kill creativity. Human creativity by nature is a wicked problem solver. It tends to use sophisticated, eclectic knowledge, which can adapt to a changing environment. Millions of years of it helped our species survive. Schools train us for the workplace, to be valuable for a market and its companies. If your market is made of tame companies, you teach kids to become tame problem solvers. Schools, and the education system in general, aim for deskilled skill sets because its structure originates from preparing children for the work in Industrial Revolution-style factories, down to the whistle blowing at the end of the class/shift. This has reached every aspect and level of education and knowledge modeling.

In his 2012 dConstruct conference speech, James Burke[10] noted that to get a permanent seat at a university one needs to find a specialization no one else understands and knows about, to make you valuable enough to give you a permanent professorship. This has put extreme limitation and niche-finding ahead of evolving.

So, when people say schools kill creativity, they mean education reduces our ability to solve wicked problems and trains us to solve tame problems.

Ford's idea, as we know, was that the intellectual or creative potential sits with the managerial layer. In *The New How,* business thinker Nilofer Merchant[11] describes the gap between management and the rest of the company as an "air sandwich"—a gap where nothing communicates well enough to be implemented efficiently. Both sides have, for a long time, disconnected, discouraging collaboration and understanding. All of this is the result of a deskilled and tame problem-shaped company structure. If things get too complex, a company structure often fails to recognize that and deal with it.

Modern managers rarely have the skills to produce the products they are managing because they never sat in the other silos. They are intermediaries between tasks' theoretical and practical aspects. With the absence of knowledge and experiential exchange, how would any manager know what steps to take to further the products or services of a company? What we see instead is the general reduction of resources, often valuable resources, and the automation of processes essential to the characteristics of a company and its brand. There is a crucial disconnect between what needs to be managed and produced and the people who execute the output of a company because single-skilled silos prevent mutual understanding between business strategy and production. A coherent end-to-end offer and synergy are blocked at an operational level.

The successful CEO who can turn around any company is a myth derived from the theory of a tame company and the reality of what wicked problems need. No CEO can tackle a wicked problem if he or she sits in a tame company. The separation between the intellectual and practical sides of a product, service, or company and its processes has halted innovation and change.

This separation expands to the customer of any product or service. Tame companies have become disconnected from them, and wicked companies are picking up those broken relationships and are making them their own.

Some educational institutions have noticed the change. MIT, a thought leader, has been calling for more cross-disciplinary or T-shaped people in their application material.

Eighteen years ago, I joined a master's degree course because it gave me a cross-disciplinary opportunity to look beyond webpages when everyone else was busy with the dot-com boom. My study colleagues and I worked first on connected devices, big data, IoT, service design, and anything we now call established and new opportunities. Our tutors and sponsors were from IDEO, MIT, Sony, and Philips. We learned about art, design, psychology, strategy, software, hardware, and human-centered research. Everyone came from a different background, and everyone had to learn something from another person's experience. Creativity and innovation were flowing.

Many of my colleagues went on to create successful and innovative companies or worked at places like Sony, Lego, or Google. I still believe that we were not particularly smarter than others, but we approached every challenge as the wicked problems they were and therefore created more progressive solutions. Everyone there had at least three skills.

Our world today has mastered mass production. Just as we have a different worldview when we are five years old, things get more complicated when we enter our teenage years. Different things matter, and we develop and use new and more complex tools. Companies need to grow up just like this. A modern workplace does not need beanbags; it needs a redefinition of what it means to learn for a lifetime. It needs to recognize and invest in multiple skills as a good thing in one worker. Why do you need a hobby when your job is complex enough?

As Esko Kilpi says, "The unintended consequence [is] that the most economical design of mass-era organizations reduces the number of skilled workers and increases the amount of less-skilled work, thus reducing costs."[12]

Now that we have robots and messengers, why do we keep reducing worker skills and knowledge, only to see them fail to solve wicked problems? Why do we try to save money buying tame tools, only to lose customers to wicked companies because our tame offer has no value anymore?

When I was working at a global ad agency, we had a project to sell for Peroni. The idea was attractive to the client, but the technologist was not invited to the meeting. Instead, the account manager, with scant knowledge about the products' realization and opportunities, met the client, then came back and asked the technologists questions. They then had issues to clarify, and the account manager fed that back to the client. This went on about three times. I never found out how the client meetings went, but the questions that came back would have taken a five-minute conversation to clarify. Only in this case, it took two weeks. The account managers tried their uninformed best, but eventually, the client left frustrated, and the agency lost the business. I have a wide variety of colleagues with similar stories, where the siloed "Chinese whisper" effect of management layers only results in unnecessary costs and kills projects.

A few years ago, General Electric's CEO reported it was embracing the future. In no small words, he announced he eradicated layers of management found unnecessary. Applying our modern tools to any business leads to the same conclusion. We don't need managers as middlemen or communicators. Wicked companies are made of lean, flat, enabled, outcome-based teams and a free flow of insights and principles.

Rachel Higham, managing director of BT IT, makes a clear statement: "For me, managers no longer exist in a modern organization. We should all be coaches. Our role is to guide, to nudge to inspire, to remove roadblocks."

We need enabled decision makers, not "Chinese whisperers." The split between the thinking and the doing, between the management layer and the "factory floor," was only the first silo. Company structures have since evolved into factories of silo mass production, and it is killing industries. More on the type and effects of silos in the next chapter.

# JUST ADD SILO!

Departments, organizational structures, and other business segments act like silos. This separation is by design and has worked for many decades. In both life and work, silos tend to harm quality and hinder understanding of problems and situations. They create friction for knowledge, synergy, and other processes vital to tackling a wicked problem. They can exist where we do not notice them or have effects we do not measure yet. This is the challenge to move from tame to wicked.

Silos exist to preserve and contain whatever their contents are. Nature is always changing, evolving, and recycling through a "grow and decay" cycle. A silo's purpose is to fight that cycle, to make it stop, or at least slow it down. This describes a grain silo but also other silos like departments, contracts, election cycles, budgets, copyrights, and so on. I am not saying all these are silos by default, but they generally are in a typical company.

Large groups are hard to manage when the outcome of an activity needs to be consistent. Since the Industrial Revolution, skills have been siloed and manager after manager has been put in place to check, report, and control processes and outcomes. Companies cloned a product a million times because this was the challenge at the time. Business units and departments have long been called silos. As the *Oxford Dictionary* puts it, a silo is "a system, process, department, et cetera that operates in isolation from others."

*Isolation* is the relevant word here, but the two use-case examples the dictionary lists are even more revealing:

"It is vital that team members step out of their **silos** and start working together."

"[as modifier] We have made significant strides in breaking down that **silo** mentality."

This shows that the negative effect of silos has been known for years, but alternatives were probably not available or perceived to be. Today is different. We have many new tools that affect every area of business. These bring options to every variation of a silo and its effects in existence.

Just think of the modern expectation of a consumer as a waterslide. Imagine if every five meters, they had to step off and get onto the next segment of the ride. That would be frustrating, deny them momentum, and defy the enjoyable purpose of the experience. Today we have tools that enable the basic delivery of a functional end-to-end service. This is starting to become the new tame.

A wicked service would be an experience. According to Pine and Gillmore's book from 1999,[13] we are living in an experience economy, beyond service, where experience is the new exponentially greater value produced for consumers.

## SKILL SILOS: THE MYTH OF THE STARTUP GENIUS

The story of a handful of entrepreneurs in a garage taking on multinationals has become more than an urban legend or a public relations exercise; it has become a small but relevant reality. The garage startup story often focuses on the genius of the founders, which enabled them to do what others were not able to do. This is misleading, omitting important facts. Many of the garage-type companies, just like many other younger companies, have tools at their disposal that big companies don't. They started as wicked companies because their baseline didn't include silos or deskilled people. Modern-day small companies can scale lean, cheaply, and fast. It does not take a genius to tackle wicked.

The gap between modern automated and enabled people who can hit moving targets and teams who can only replicate other's work is nearly a generation wide. The narratives to explain it have unfortunately been as uninformed as their storytellers. Some are so uncritical of technology and the people behind it that it reminds one of Arthur C. Clarke's laws, and this one in particular: "Any sufficiently advanced technology is indistinguishable from magic."

If you look at the way startup founders are bathed in money and companies have been looking at specialists and novelty technology as silver bullets, it is clear that someone does believe in magic or miracles. A balanced assessment of opportunity has been replaced by a fear of losing out and by investment greed. The startup genius was a simplistic narrative, yet few of the prominent dot-com leaders are geniuses or innovators. Most of them are just more competitive, took more risks, or stole from smarter people. It is worth having a look at one of the more prominent examples to see how much this can be true or not true.

Let us look at Facebook. Mark Zuckerberg originally built a web scraper to skim university student pages. Most developers at the time could do so. He then stole the actual idea of a social website from the Winklevoss twins, no genius there. You might even wonder how much he would have been able to scale it if Sean Parker had not approached him and shaped the university project into a company. As Zuckerberg himself says, "Sean was pivotal in helping Facebook transform from a college project into a real company."[14]

Furthermore, social platforms were already around if you remember Friendster, Myspace, and Orkut. So the idea was neither new nor a genius stroke. What made Facebook so powerful were the tools it were using and the fact that it was providing deconstructed narratives in the form of posting images and small messages and the critical status update. No genius here, just contemporary tools.

Computer code created those new tools, and many of the early founders were computer coders at heart, but since the dot-com boom, we have had a lot of computer coders around. It's just that many have been kept in silos, unable to apply their thinking and being asked to use a minimal set of their skill capacity and creativity. In over twenty years, I have seen many people with technology skills kept in a little corner somewhere, surrounded by a company structure unable to use their skills—a structure that kept their ideas tame. Many were eventually leaving industries never to come back, not wanting to work any longer for people who did not understand the new paradigm or appreciate their skills and mindsets.

Today we can equip individuals with everything from detailed data analytics to website and content managing or business financial tools. Two years ago, I managed a smart city tech Kickstarter campaign called The Things Network by myself. Within thirty days, we reached forty-seven countries and 180 cities and closed at over 200 percent of what we were aiming for. The Things Network is now probably one of the most active internet-of-things communities in the world.

Individuals can now use their multiple skills or learn them more quickly because tools enable them to do so. All this lets us tackle wicked problems with small teams of enabled multi-skilled people. This has slashed the number of people it needs for a productive team to be successful. Companies are reducing the number of people they have and hope for more productivity to come from it, but unless their people can use multiple skills and reach beyond silos, this extra value will not manifest. Tools only show the synergetic benefit that startups have shown in the right context.

Innovation does not need specialists, but it needs to let people flow beyond silos.

## LANGUAGE SILOS: SPECIALIST LANGUAGE AND BELIEF SYSTEMS

Language is both beautiful and deadly. It can move countries into war. Ask me; I'm German. Words have immense power in leading ideas, nudging behavior, and forming actions and justifications for activities. They can convince people to kill each other for reasons not their own.

As Hitler's commander, Hermann Goering, famously said during the Nuremberg trials, "All you have to do is tell them they are being attacked and denounce the pacifists for lack of patriotism and exposing the country to danger . . . It works the same in every country."

Take the words "freedom fighter" and "terrorist." Depending on which one you use or hear, philosophy and politics will shift your actions quite differently. Most professions have similar terminology that reveals the way they see the world.

Now before we go too dark and deep, let us go back to the lighter side of the same effect.

Professions create silos via language. Language can create clarity, but when power and politics enter the equation, language is often used artificially to stop up the flow of information or discourse.

Companies have played this game for many years. The fact that people need a defined job title to justify their position is shaping other people's perception and restrictions on how information should flow. Some companies have developed a secret language existing of hundreds of acronyms. Most find this unnecessary and confusing. Some of the proven downsides of abbreviations in companies are:[15]

- Confusion and alienation of listeners.
- Mistakes and disagreements based on false interpretations listeners may make.
- Cheapened perceived value of products, solutions, and services.

A few years back, when I was working at an advertising agency with a range of Procter & Gamble brands as their clients, I discovered P&G language. The first few meetings with the client were fascinating. Specific industry terms that everyone was familiar with had been renamed for reasons I am yet trying to understand.[16]

- **AMJ:** April, May, June, or P&G's fiscal third quarter
- **CBD:** Customer business development, which other companies might call *sales.*
- **ER:** External relations, known elsewhere as *public relations.*

Philosophers have long had a habit of using terminologies in a set context. This makes philosophy very inaccessible, as ideas reference ideas, making it necessary to read multiple books to understand the first book. This cryptic puzzle makes for a more accurate conversation, but it creates a threshold for a more open flow of knowledge. If you are tackling a wicked problem, friction slows you down and makes you less competitive. Jake Knapp's Google design sprints do not have unique language or tools. They add value because they are as accessible as it gets (more on this later).

Inaccessibility is friction. Businesses don't need friction.

Through my career, I could see that software engineers, designers, strategists, enterprise architects, business analysts, and others used words that could mean different things, depending on the profession of the speaker: *model, artifact, tool.* All this adds hours of friction and potential failures to a project. As wicked projects rely on interdisciplinary conversations, collision of languages is inevitable. We need something better.

The opposite phenomenon is to use different terminologies in different industries for the same thing. One example would be the advertising industry using the term *integrated marketing* for user or customer experiences that use different channels or, as other industries would call it, different *interactive content platforms,* to create an interconnected and seamless experience. The television industry picked up on the same type of idea and called it *transmedia* or *transmedia storytelling.*

Any language tries to describe reality just about well enough to find and possibly map the truths within it that matter. A nation's language represents how its culture describes the world. No language gives a complete description of reality, and we should recognize this. This means we should allow thoughts and ideas from other professions to mix with the ones we know and always be open to a more complete way to describe things.

A language is a tool. Think about tools like an axe. An axe is a very versatile tool that can work wood in many ways. However, sometimes a drill will do better. You could probably take down a tree with an electric drill and make some holes with an axe, but the results are very different. Combining both tools will get you infinitely further.

Not all languages have words that can do the same. This means different meanings should be part of your toolset. This, in turn, says we should not stick to one silo or language to solve a wicked problem.

Language is a powerful anchor and silo from which to break free. When I first moved to London, my English was not that good. My course consisted of half native English speakers and the other half of students for whom English was a second language. I was not the only one struggling.

Interestingly, it was harder for an English speaker to understand my English than it was for a non-English speaker. It was the same English, and the non-English speaker had fewer skills to follow me, so why would he or she understand me more? I assume that if you are more flexible in what you might consider as right or wrong, you can be more open to information and you can interpret information better. If all you have ever known is one language, you are not flexible enough to see alternatives right in front of you.

In transformation or innovation projects, a common language is becoming one of the most valuable tools to establish. We are living in a cross-disciplinary work environment with cross-functional teams. Maybe we need a meta-language everyone can agree on.

## BUDGET SILOS: WHEN MONEY IS IN A TIME LOCK

Business planning and strategy are good things. Planning puts activities and processes into perspective. It helps one evaluate, focus, and prioritize, just before reality eats up everything. More importantly, it can shape a vision, goal, or target to aim for and agree upon, even though this might change multiple times along the journey. In general, creating fixed points in the future is beneficial.

However, planning tends to lock up budgets in time-based silos. This, in turn, makes the flow of investment very fixed within a company. We are now living in a world where product cycles are continually decreasing. Automotive companies still need around three to four years to bring a new car to market. Kickstarter hardware projects often build things from scratch in about 18 months. *From scratch,* in this case, means no company even exists when they start. Software-based startups can create a so-called MVP (minimum viable product) in an average of three to six months. Other innovation sprints aim for under three months from a possible piece of data and an assumption to a prototype or first-pass business case.

For a faster turnaround, a Google sprint mapped on some of IDEO's design thinking takes a single week. Many of those cycles today contain business cases within their design or concept cycle. This fast-paced iteration means that some projects will need extra boosts of the budget if specific iterations require it. Preassigned and fixed budgets or sign-off processes stifle great ideas and impact; they cannot compete in a world where deconstruction has created iterative budgets and funding systems. I will show some examples in a later chapter of deconstructed budgets with a much lower risk and higher impact than traditional ways of planning on how to spend your money.

The fact that the flow of money into projects by itself is hindered is a significant factor for businesses to evolve from tame to wicked.

## IN-SILO POLARIZATION

The effect of social polarization is well understood and can easily be observed. It has a significant impact on innovation and flexibility, on thought and action.

Silos are meant to preserve what works, reducing the risk of failure. Businesses set up silos and will define a risk level acceptable to each. If change is a risk—and it always is—then, by definition, silos will move even further away from that risk. The extremist effect of a silo or social group, therefore, is lowering the flexibility of its group members. This means it takes additional energy or investment just to keep a silo aligned with the business level of risk-taking and change. Wicked companies deconstruct and minimize risk. Having fewer silos reduces friction and therefore the investment needed to stay flexible and agile as a company. Change and disruption happen when these silo characteristics are deconstructed and removed.

As Tim O'Reilly noted in his book *WTF?*[17], Apple used to have a history of secrecy. They had to adopt transparency because people don't accept the silos anymore and it made them flourish as a company.

The bottom-line effect here is that silos will tend to progress toward easier goals for themselves. This means the less siloed a company gets, the more likely it will be agile and competitive. The opposite example would be modern-day politics and social media, which have polarized nations. This makes solving problems nearly impossible, and it needs to change drastically. It also shows that the internet has the same political silo effect as politics itself. Your company would not do well to eradicate or ignore alternative views; they might be your next solution and revenue stream.

# ZERO FRICTION

I f our new tools gave us anything, it is the ability to reduce friction to zero. If the consumer expects anything, it is a frictionless path toward their need.

Friction is an increase in the energy needed for a process output to be created. If it did not exist, a moving object would continuously move without continually having to add energy. Friction exists in many processes and activities. Business or social silos create it. By breaking down silos, we can reduce it and increase efficiency. Zero friction should be everyone's aim for every aspect of the business, extended all the way and including the customer.

Companies have always tried to increase productivity and efficiency after producing an initial product. They move their factories close to where the materials ship to reduce transport costs. The automotive industry has famously introduced the "just-in-time" concept, where materials and components are never stored. Parts are delivered just when they are needed, reducing costs of storage and the building of storage facilities.

No trading happens in the New York Stock Exchange anymore. The actual transactions occur in a building that sits closer to the internet backbone cable. This shaves off microseconds, and lets trade data travel faster and increases gains.

New ecosystems of timekeeping and communication made all of this possible. Today, we can go to a website, book a ticket, call a cab, and be on a plane in mere hours; all paid electronically. We don't need to go to a bank to pick up money or a travel agent to book the tickets for us. This new way of moving people and goods accelerated at the turn of the twentieth century, when Jules Verne wrote many of his now-famous science-fiction stories about flying to the moon, exploring the deep sea, or traveling around the world in only eighty days. Without timetables, global timekeeping, or reliable transport, planning a voyage around the world was a seemingly impossible task. Steamboats and new train routes connected more places around the world, but without synchronized time or normalized timetables, it was hard to predict and plan the connection between, for example, goods arriving in a harbor and the train arriving to pick them up for the next part of the voyage. Verne realized the innovation that timetables represented and estimated that in the future, someone could travel the world within eighty days. Little did he know that a journalist called Nellie Bly would do this only sixteen years later in just over seventy-two days.

Today, we find ourselves in the next step of a transition that started during the Industrial Revolution. The frictionless flow of data and products has become a commodity. Many businesses have experienced the latter, but are still working on the former. Because the tame problem of creating both products or data and getting them where they should go is a commodity now, business and customer value is established above that level. Customers and the market expect infrastructure and technology inching closer and closer to zero friction. And they now expect more.

Being a tame company will make it very hard for you to go beyond the zero-friction bottom line. When trying to tackle the wicked problems of today, your real friction will reduce the value of your product or service so much that you won't be able to compete or convert a customer.

We have personalized automation, communication, and other data channels with capabilities unheard of in past generations. The quantitative or efficiency aspect of a company does not create the margin, value, or differentiator anymore. The fact that the luxury industry wants hyper-luxury should have signaled to everyone that people expect what has previously been only available to high-income parts of the population: decide to go to Paris and fly there within a few hours, know the name of your driver, get a personal trainer for lunch at the click of a button, order things within the hour, create and upload a movie you made yourself, get funding for any project you could think up. No friction there.

Zero friction is a way to envisage this new world, where people's abilities and knowledge are magnified through a free flow of information and opportunities. It will take a wicked team and wicked companies to find the new complex ways in which we can offer new services, experiences, and whatever lies beyond.

In the next chapter, I will show how what we once produced in a tame way started to become deconstructed and wicked. From code to the internet, because the mindset shifted, the world followed. Connectedness, the illegality of copyright infringement, personal data, and new currencies are all just symptoms of the fact that we have moved beyond bespoke industrialization. We face challenges and opportunities that a tame company cannot solve. Time to get wicked.

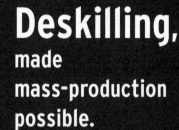

**Deskilling,**
made
mass-production
possible.

It shaped the way
we are still designing
companies today.

Today's opportunities
are horizontal. Deskilling
is vertical and diminishes
value in every company.

enry Ford, 1863 – 1947

# PART II

# OOPS, I DID IT AGAIN!

**From tame to wicked.**

# THE MINDSET-TOOL-WORLD FEEDBACK LOOP

When we are describing innovation or the creation of new tools and inventions, we often focus on the technology used or the genius of the sole inventor. It is a familiar narrative to simplify causality and purpose onto a single entity or thing. But life, as they say, is a bit more complicated. For some reason, things that come in three seem to land well within our mind, so I will start with a cycle with three parts. This cycle has likely been running for thousands of years, but it is good to bring it back into memory. It is that cycle that wicked companies have integrated into their ways of working and problem solving. Tame companies do not have this cycle and can't evolve. This cycle is made of *mindset, tool,* and *world.*

**MINDSET:** Thinking shapes the way we see and interpret the world; it makes sense of it and the way we set up our actions. Thinking creates ideas: many that we drop or forget, others that we put into actions. Thinking starts and ends within a context. We continuously test ideas with the outside world to prove what is part of our reality and what is not. When we are looking about or "scan a room," we gather information and start examining what we are considering the context to be. Within ourselves, we set opportunities and restrictions. This is an organic process. Based on that, we behave differently in different social groups and contexts. We don't laugh at a funeral, and we don't boo in a movie theater, even if the film is awful. Mindsets are amazingly powerful in the way they can expand our reality, and they can be utterly vicious in the way they can restrict our actions. In my twenty years of innovation and transformation, I have found people's mindset their biggest ally and biggest foe.

**TOOLS:** Tools—or products and services—are the manifested artifacts of our actions. Human-made fire, housing, the wheel, movable type, penicillin, airplanes, and mobile phones are all tools with a purpose. It is unusual to call a house a tool, but in this context, I will call it a tool which protects you from weather and other dangers.

Many of our tools are cultural: we build houses differently in different countries. You would not find a shower box that uses electricity to heat the water in Germany. Japanese toilets are very different from the standard ones in other countries, some of which have bidets. Some people prefer their main social gatherings to happen in their kitchen; others favor the living room as the primary social space.

We track history sometimes as a list of scientific achievements, or sometimes by the invention of tools because they have such an effect on culture and society's events. Imagine if the Spanish did not have their metal armor when they went to South America. It is our current favorite narrative, the narrative of tools—or technology—as the primary driver. However, if everyone can afford the same tools these days, why isn't this narrative more openly challenged? It is essential to understand that technology is already a commodity. If you are still defining your business value by the number of engineers you employ or the servers you run, you are not going to survive the next phase.

**WORLD:** Many believe that behavior is based on context and follows from a combination of the present thinking and the tools available. In the legal system, we consider circumstances, not just black-and-white actions. This means the whole world acts as the feedback space. For example, whenever I dance, I think about in what way it would be appropriate to dance, given the music, location, and whom I am with. I don't know about you, but I dance differently in front of my child than I would in front of clients with whom I might go out for a night. Most of our actions follow this principle. The world around us does matter. Where you are born, where you are right now is playing a big part is what you might do next. For both problems and solutions, the world is an unforgiving entity that, as I heard, eats strategy for breakfast.

Tools have been given too much attention. An excellent example of how tools alone can fail when mindset and world are not attended is an app called Slack. Slack was celebrated as an excellent replacement for email, but has accumulated the same messy problems that email has. Why? Because of mindset and world leading people to use it in confusing and spammy ways. One must pay attention to all three aspects to complete the cycle and be able to evolve.

**INTERDEPENDENCIES:** The significant new cycle that we are experiencing today started around the 1960s. What is fascinating is how this new cycle could ingrain itself across all three of its aspects.

Individuals can't achieve success by themselves, nor do their ideas exist in a vacuum. Their surroundings always influence and inspire them. The same is true for our tools. Even ideas that lead to great tools can take a long time to find the right context to manifest. Think of the scientists and inventors thrown into prison because their ideas conflicted with their surroundings at the time. Even today, inventors and entrepreneurs move countries to find the best context for their ideas, a phenomenon known as human capital flight, brain drain, or brain gain, depending on which country is measuring it.

Most historical examples of the world affecting output involved religious, racial, and/or political prosecution. A more recent case of this is the closure of the famous Bauhaus in Weimar, Germany. A study from the American Economic Association elaborates on how German Jewish emigrés boosted U.S. innovation.[18] Substantial threats like prosecution do not always drive those migrations. Smaller migrations result more from a pull than a push: sometimes incentives and opportunities are enough to make people move away from their homeland.

I have lived in London for twenty years. My main reason for coming here was to join a course at the Royal College of Art in 2000. I had seen the work people were doing there and it connected with my ideas and ambitions. I had not seen the mindset at this college anywhere else. At the time, one of my best friends offered me the chance to start a company with him. I had been building websites throughout the dot-com boom. I had other plans than to keep building websites. I never looked back.

London is one of those places that is driven by its migrants. I have never seen a place that has more countries traveling through it nor one with a more diverse and inclusive mix of mindsets, which creates a world where anything can happen. There are similarly attractive places, though: Boston with its MIT; Silicon Valley for technology companies; Paris and London for fashion; and some outlier cities or locations outperform for different reasons, like Groningen, which had 10 percent of Deloitte's Fast 50 growing companies despite having only 200,000 inhabitants.[19]

Even within the technology and the startup world, some places are better than others. London is known for FinTech or financial industry startups. Barcelona is known for smart-city technology startups. Decentralized or crowdsourced startups seem to align less with the London community. When I managed a Dutch startup, The Things Network's Kickstarter campaign, its decentralized smart-city hardware spread across thirty-six countries and 130 cities in only a month. It has now grown to over 500 communities worldwide, but the UK hardly picked up on it. The Netherlands, Germany, and South America over-indexed.

There are maker communities in all countries, but the way they pick up on various tools depends on their perception of what is valuable. Tools themselves are not siloed indicators of success or adoption, yet businesses often act as if installing the latest version of Microsoft Office will magically improve productivity.

Starbucks had great success in many countries. The Italians hated it even though its coffee culture inspired it. According to Statista, Starbucks owns 27,339 stores around the globe in over 60 countries.[20] On several occasions, it announced its intention to open a shop in Italy, yet it took 47 years for the company to make its way into Italian culture, in September 2018. The next decade or so will prove if Italian behavior is finally ready to accept Starbucks.

QR codes are another example of the world affecting the use of tools. Having been very successful in Japan, they failed in the West. The technology existed in both parts of the globe, but in Japan, people had QR code readers preinstalled on their phone. In the U.S. and Europe, readers were freely available, but many people had never come across them and did not bother to download them. They therefore never reached the widespread adoption they had in Japan.

• • •

Some ideas reappear every few years, die, and then suddenly stay and grow because their feedback cycle is finally right. Many of Leonardo da Vinci's designs were famously ahead of their time. The Wright brothers were working out of their garage with little or no money. At the same time, a highly funded project, including many accomplished and well-paid engineers, was trying to invent the first functioning flying machine. The highly funded team failed, some argue because of the wrong mindset; the Wright brothers made history.

The electric car disappeared in the mid-1990s, but saw a revival in the 2010s. VR has been tried for a few decades, but Facebook has cancelled its Oculus lab—maybe it needs another decade.

This is why problems today are wicked. One needs to understand all three aspects and investigate if they all click. We have been sold the idea that a tool—or technology—alone solves our complex problems. Thinking and behavior have been ignored in this narrative for too long and have set up many projects and companies for failure. Let's be smarter.

## A FEW MORE DETAILS TO CONFUSE YOU

It is widely understood that the adoption of a product or service is of high relevance. Creating adoption is an art form. Unfortunately, the narrative that novelty or feature richness of a technology-based tool will set it up for success is as widespread as it is false. Behavior can give a much better indication of the readiness of your customers to adopt.

For example, the threshold of a person to join others in the same action can have an immense impact on a situation and its outcome, not unlike the famous butterfly effect, where a small starting point can have an exponentially more significant result. In *Everything is Obvious*,[21] Duncan J. Watts explains how a news story can have a completely different spin based on minimal differences in its real characteristics. He compares two villages with the same people and identical context, with the only difference being one person having a slightly lower threshold to act on its context. He describes a group of angry workers, none of whom is revolting or acting violently. Most people in the group need to observe others in revolt to make the decision to revolt themselves. Only one person does not need anyone else to act as that trigger. In his example, one village has that person starting a riot, the other one, without that person taking action, has no riot.

The sharing economy is an excellent concept, and it is comfortable to build a transaction platform now, years after Amazon and eBay have led the way. But the simple example of borrowing a drill from a neighbor and the surrounding behavior shows how fallible the idea is. Maybe the mainstream approach of people sharing more is the wrong approach. Perhaps the founders of those companies should deconstruct the world aspect into a smaller one, or look for the right one.

Thinking, tools, and behavior are interdependent parts. One follows the other in an endless, iterative cycle. Ignoring one of them creates an incomplete cycle; this is likely to result in at least unnecessary costs if not outright failure for any change or project because adoption or profitability will not be high enough.

I used this metaphor for the last twenty years when looking at technology and companies ever since the dot-com boom started to focus on technology. Looking at the mindset and world frequently gave me a complete picture of what I was looking at. The more we know of our world or any other aspect, the lower risks we will face and the less we will be overwhelmed.

The internet of things is one emerging industry too heavily focused on the technology or tool aspect of the solution. Sigfox and The Things Network are competitors whose focus is on large-scale deployment to reach critical mass. They expect large numbers will create the first relevant commercial benefit and case study. They have not yet evolved beyond the silo mindset of engineers and makers, who are generally focused on the tools themselves. Their communities are not set up to consider the behavior that will create the case studies which will evolve the relevance of this new technology. Like many other internet-of-things projects, they are stuck on projects like plant moisture sensors. The innovation will likely come from outside this silo.

Facebook was not the best social network ever, nor was it the first. Orkut led the way before Facebook in some countries, and it survived for a very long time in South America. One of Facebook's benefits was that it had colleges and universities as a backdrop, which created a consistent funnel of new users for the platform. At the time, colleges would be Myspace- or Facebook-dominated. People did not use one or the other because it was the better platform, but because their friends were on it. The world drove the demand, not the excellence or features of the tool. The tool had already become a commodity among students.

Science fiction has for some time been inspired inventions. Consider the sci-fi story the thinking, and imaginations the tools. What the best science fiction does is not just to describe a tool, but to elaborate on the behavior associated with it. Science fiction had done this long before *Minority Report* inspired gesture-driven interfaces. As a medium or communication channel, it has accelerated positive thinking and has given examples of which behavior to align with once the tools it described would be in existence. This means communications can have a significant impact on mindset and the world. If you are running a change or transformation project, don't underestimate that.

Jules Verne's *Around the World in Eighty Days* is a beautiful example of a story that shows the connection between thinking, tools, and behavior. The main protagonist, Phileas Fogg, is a man without any background, or at least any background known to anyone. He is described as someone who does not behave like a human but like an automaton, a clockwork devoid of human emotions.

He represents a change of behavior through the tools that appeared around the time when the book was written. The story gives a balanced look at the upsides and downsides of technology on human behavior. The upside is to be able to travel around the world faster than ever. The downside is that the human using those tools—in the book, Phileas Fogg uses universal timekeeping and modern modes of transport like steamships—will lose his humanity or perception of the beauty of the world around him. However he risks his relationship with technology by stopping his race around the world to save an Indian princess from certain death, showing that there is the hope that technology will not eradicate our emotions.

Companies and consultancies are slowly noticing that what worked in the past is not working any longer, but they are stuck in the same siloed approach as everyone else. Their strategy has slowly shifted from merely dropping new solutions—tools—onto companies and their people to a more human-centered approach toward change. If you consider people, you find the world aspect. Many companies are stuck on the tool level and need to bring in mindset and world.

When I was working with a prominent automotive brand on an electric vehicle project, obstacles existed in all three areas. The company hadn't embraced the new thinking of modern multi-modal transport, the tools were out of date, and the behavior was locked in a process that Henry Ford had started, and which most automotive companies had driven right into a dead end. After we presented the concept and prototype, the first comment the vice president gave was, "We need a completely new set of partners." Their world and existing partner's mindset and tools were not ready.

When the MIT Media Lab had laboratories in Dublin, the tool focus was evident. I worked there in 2002, and we had only two departments looking at thinking and behavior instead of tools. Nicholas Negroponte, the genius founder behind the Media Lab, came to Dublin and scrapped those departments. They were primarily looking at what is now called social media, service design, and big data. His focus on tools made the opportunities invisible to him.

"Have a great product, and they will come" has never been a better guarantee of failure.

Since the Industrial Revolution, tools have been king. We removed the mindset and limited the behavior of people engaging with the system. People were only fillers for what machines couldn't do yet. Now that our tools can mass-produce without human help, we need to let people think again. Consumers already do; so should everyone in a company. A company that does not align its mindset with the rest of the world will make all the wrong decisions.

Over the last few decades, a couple of mindset-tool-world feedback loops have been developing. They are fewer than you might think, but some are still evolving.

# OBJECT-ORIENTED PROGRAMMING: YOUR BRAIN IN 1,000 NUTSHELLS

Some cultural shifts are more significant than others. Mindset, tool, and world are the three components in a cycle that has existed since we first created tools. The components are interdependent. Our society has focused on the tool aspect of the current cycle. The mindset and world feedback, however, are less understood and must be understood if we are to progress effectively. This might be one of the reasons why industries and other cultural systems are collapsing and being questioned. While we are busy believing in connected tools, everything else has become somewhat deconstructed.

Back in the '60s and '70s, some brilliant people came up with a new approach to how computer code should be structured. Early code was linear, like the way we perceive time: one action after another. The code would start executing at the top and ran down line-by-line to the end—a single timeline. I am simplistic here, but mostly a piece of software was one large chunk of code.

Software inevitably became more extensive and more complex. Hundreds of lines of code turned into thousands. Projects that previously could be produced by a single coder turned into team efforts. This increase in size made it more and more challenging to plan, structure, and develop software projects. Even worse, when code failed, it was not always easy to detect why and where, because the whole code package was one big black box. To debug or to find the problem, programmers had to go through those thousands of lines of code. The bigger the projects became, the more inefficient linear coding became.

To tackle complexity, code needed to become more flexible. A combination of challenges led to one of the most significant evolutions in computer code design. It was called object-oriented programming (OOP).[22]

The idea was simple, yet genius: separate every software functionality into an object or class. One object takes care of the mouse input: one takes care of the screen display; one the internet connection; and so on. Objects could be small. Some would take care of a video play button functionality, contain the stream of a video or other data; some held a floating-point number rather than an integer of a number. This deconstructed computer code and its capabilities, but more importantly, it created new thinking among coders. From then on, coders began solving every problem by deconstructing its context. OOP revolutionized the industry and shifted a mindset. It made many complex systems more understandable, structured, and replicable.

By using objects that used self-sufficient code, you could reuse many hours of work in other projects by reusing the objects: a video player, a screen display, managing mouse input, and so on. If you produced it once, you never had to do it again. This made code very reusable and accelerated production significantly. It also made it easier to find errors, as a video error would be in the video object, not somewhere spread across all of the code.

Tools and mindset influence how we look at the world. Programmers started to look at the world the way they structured their code, as collections of objects. From that moment on, any project would begin by breaking a possible context into its logical objects, then starting to create those objects in code and wiring or connecting them into a functional program or application. The first step was always to deconstruct the context of the needed design. As coders created more solutions for our new software-driven reality, they looked visually and experientially expressed our reality through a deconstructed and object-oriented lens. Are you still wondering why someone came up with messages reduced into 140 or 280 characters?

I remember moving from linear script languages like BASIC and HTML into object-oriented ones. My brain hurt for a month, but it was worth it.

Let me give you an example of how a programmer's mind looks at a problem. Imagine a bicycle. Let's say it is made of rubber wheels and a metal frame. In OOP, you would create a metal and a rubber object. You would then create two-wheel objects from the rubber object, and a bicycle frame object out of the metal object, a process called *inheritance* that lets you use objects with similar properties and expand their characteristics. This means I could use a metal object to create a screw object, a gun object, a tee-bar object, or a bicycle frame object. So I had the bicycle frame and two-wheel objects. I might want to put a chain on the frame and pedals and add air to the wheels, but I had a very simple bike already. Separating something into its objects is a bit like dividing them into functional aspects of a bigger picture.

On a more complex project like a car, OOP coders would start by taking the car apart: the engine, the wheels, the paint job, the seats, the material that covered the seats. The vehicle is made out of many components. This might sound simplistic, but coders, through OOP, became manufacturers and product designers. In so doing, they began creating every element of anything they looked at as an object in itself which they could use and reuse. Because our culture interacts with software and its capabilities a lot, we started to see an object-oriented way of being able to interact and to behave around the way software was structured. Object by object, linear things split into single, interdependent objects. For years, computer code was like a movie script. Now it has become a LEGO set, and we are still building with it.

OOP has become the standard programming paradigm of our times. Even younger programming languages like Adobe's ActionScript and JavaScript have embraced it: its power to reuse existing objects and therefore save hours of coding work is too large a production benefit. Knowing where your problem sits by knowing which object creates an issue is a huge time saver. When a new coder joins the team, they can start with a small object, and step by step get familiar with the broader system. This is a sustainable way to run and evolve projects.

The reality of code is more complicated, but the essence lies in this principle of structuring it. I grew up with the BASIC computer language on a Commodore 64, one of the first available home computers. BASIC was still structured linearly. This was my first computer code experience. Only much later through Flash ActionScript and other languages like Objective-C did I discover OOP. The shift your mind has to make to access such a deconstructed system is overwhelming at first. Once you get used to it, it is a beautiful and practical system, one that might make you wonder why no one structured things like it earlier.

Through a new model like OOP, the open source movement was possible. How can you avoid everyone working on the same file at the same time and the conflicts that come with that? Deconstruct it into many pieces that don't interfere with each other when updated. If you deconstruct and let a billion people improve modules without interfering with each other, how useful and advanced can your system get? Furthermore, OOP deconstructed geography too, removing the need for a massive company with thousands of people in one place.

For a long time, companies have benefited from outsourcing modules and bigger pieces of their infrastructure to save costs.

This outsourcing makes solutions, and their modules, often siloed. Relying on those outsourced pieces of infrastructure and know-how can create dependencies that reduce companies' agility. Now that we can deconstruct projects so much, you must find a balance between the value you want to own and control and the value you can outsource and depend on as a business.

I like to think of outsourcing as a silo wrapper around a deconstruction principle. If you are deconstructing, you can still maintain the knowledge within your system. If you outsource, you often give it away, and it can become a value you pay for rather than create revenue from—a liability rather than an asset.

During my time at the Science Museum in London, we created a new integrated content delivery platform across departments involving the institution's CMS, or content management software. Sitecore, the CMS of choice, was managed by a third-party partner. For our solution, we needed new ways to connect to the CMS and new data request calls. It was minimal work for a developer. In our case, however, it became a liability, affecting our timelines and budget. If the institution could have anticipated that improving the ecosystem would be a constant, iterative effort to assure innovation, maybe the partnership should have been different or the CMS management should have been in-house.

Tools in a company should be used in their most effective way. This means they should be flexible. Unfortunately, most solutions don't provide this flexibility or customization. There is a business incentive to lock companies into enterprise software solutions. This is not sustainable. Friction with other systems and lack of bespoke features create additional costs. Software by its nature can be very flexible; it is businesses that have slowed down innovation by locking capabilities into silos and adding costs for their straightforward improvements.

Modern software is amazingly powerful: able to be deconstructed and connect to a thousand systems and other capabilities. Profits and upselling have diminished this potential. It is like building a speedboat to drive it in a pond.

When I created a new content delivery platform and framework for one of London's largest museums, all the parts were designed to be customizable and expandable just like the code that created them. Right after launch, we were able to use it for another exhibition, and it saved weeks in development time. This was many years ago. Today, it takes a few hours to set up an API (application programming interface) which is, in the simplest terms, a publicly accessible object or set of objects that everyone can use across the internet. Companies like Google and Amazon have significant parts of their business built on these publicly accessible objects and groups of functionality, which they sell as a service. Accessible code is big business.

We live in a world where software is everywhere. More importantly, we live in a world where software and our world are deconstructed first and connected second. Modern, successful companies are built around deconstructed parts of functionality that populate valuable sets of products and services.

This is the LEGO set everyone is playing with. If you want to participate or contribute, if you want to be relevant and agile, you have to consider every aspect of your business.

The deconstructed thinking and tools are not invisible anymore. There is a reason Facebook's timeline is a list of deconstructed messages and content objects. There is a reason Airbnb deconstructed hotels and every other home into available rooms. There is a reason Bitcoin uses thousands of server "objects" to construct a new currency. There is a reason Napster broke down record albums into individual songs.

The internet itself did not become a scalable success because it could connect some computers. It became scalable by deconstructing a single data package between two computers into smaller pieces.

Coders create our world, and this is how coders look at the world and translate it into solutions—deconstructed into objects.

However, it is easy to mistake deconstructed thinking for ideas like decentralization or externalization. It is not that, and I will elaborate on the differences in the following chapters.

When I expanded my design skills and started to be a coder, I instantly recognized the similarity between the mindsets. The underlying principle of design deconstruction or destruction—atomization or disassembly of a problem into its logical parts to create a new solution—is taught to most design students. It is hard to see this mindset at work because, in most design work, we only see the final product. But ask any designer if you could have a look in their sketch or workbook, and you would see the logical aspects and how they work on tackling bits and pieces before putting them back together into an entirely new design. Have a look at a modern coder's project, and you will see thousands of objects that are the parts of his or her thinking, doing the same thing.

The takeaway from this is that deconstruction is more substantially important than connectivity. If you connect more things to your non-deconstructed business, your business value will not travel across the network. It will be a speedboat in a pond. You will be stuck in a tame and linear way of looking at and solving problems.

We live in a deconstructed new reality. It is everywhere. Its higher complexity seems overwhelming for tame and linear thinkers. It looks exciting and full of opportunities for wicked thinkers. You can be tame, or you can be wicked.

## IT'S THE INTERNET, STUPID!

The internet's success did not come just from connecting computers or fostering e-commerce. It deconstructed network connections to become as scalable and as robust as it is today. But because our attempts to understand it got it a bit wrong, anything that came after was hard to process.

The internet's origin lies in a decentralized approach to computer power—a deconstructed solution to a sizeable problem. It began when a couple of people tried to timeshare computer processes to create more significant number-crunching power and capabilities, to increase what was possible at the time with a single machine.

But when transmitting data between two machines, the connection had to be always on until all of the data was transferred. This was not scalable.

The idea that solved this was "package-switching,"[24] which meant transmitting data between multiple computers by deconstructing each data delivery into small packages. This would also affect network issues like dropped data and bandwidth fluctuations. In a network where roads, connections, and the ecosystem are not reliable, having only a single route between A and B carries too high a risk of failure. The smart idea was to have those packages pick alternative routes to get from A to B. If one of the roads was obstructed or broken, the package could choose another route. Our Uber drivers have many alternative routes now, based on traffic density and live data coming from Google and other data resources. The system is not too dissimilar to what made the internet a successful idea.

Thus it was deconstruction, not connectivity, that made the internet grow. Because these early ideas were based on deconstruction, deconstruction became a favorite way for engineers to think.

The ability to move information freely in any way is the essence of what modern networks and systems are great at. Every idea since then has been about a coder deconstructing parts of reality and aligning them with this paradigm to make use of this very characteristic of the internet and grow a new value in this new economy. Deconstruction is a little like turning water into steam. The energy added to make the molecules move more will change their inherent abilities.

The first time mainstream media and the economy took note of the internet was when shops appeared on it as e-commerce. Most of the time, established companies just put newspapers on websites.

The lack of a deconstructed mindset made the dot-com boom very inefficient in its value production. The present has always used the past to interpret the future until a new mindset was understood. The analogy of "faster horses versus cars" comes to mind.

Most new paradigms are treated and explored based on existing standards. The media narrative quickly focused what little sense it could make of this new internet on the fact that computers were connected. *Connectivity* was the word. This simple narrative has still not been rectified to include the *deconstruction* aspect needed to make use of the internet in the way it is most effective.

Established companies have maintained their silos and siloed products and have wasted nearly two decades without a deconstructed mindset. We all thought we could add the single characteristic of connectivity to our businesses. This means many companies kept very release-driven, rather than iterative, ways of producing and updating new products and services. Most new efforts kept being locked in the same silos.

Sir Tim Berners-Lee, the inventor of the internet, has focused his recent efforts on open data. He understands like no one else that if the availability of data is not open and deconstructed, it will stifle the internet and all of society substantially. It will take more people than the inventors of the internet to clarify the path ahead.

Business is still in large parts based on artificial scarcity and locking customers into service ecosystems. This restriction is counter to how a network creates value. In a network, data has to first flow without friction, and value is generated via usage of the network and its data. The connectivity and deconstruction narratives are a decisive factor for business benefit or loss.

If you can connect a million more people to your product or service, you will create a linear increase in revenue. If you deconstruct tools and services so your customers can produce the product or parts of the service themselves, your growth will be exponential.

A connected approach without deconstruction creates a

linear revenue increase. A deconstructed approach can create an exponential opportunity. This difference is the difference between tame and wicked.

I am not sure if Facebook or Google understood the potential and underlying characteristics of what they were building. Zuckerberg, like any other coder, has an object-oriented and deconstructed view of the world, so there wasn't an innovative mind behind that either. Google did spend tremendous efforts on creating an API for many of their services, which was a vast deconstructed opportunity. Facebook focused on advertising, so it was very tame on the level of growth.

It is hard to say if the internet was further influencing the deconstructed nature of OOP or if OOP influenced the internet. The difference might be irrelevant. What is clear is that the mainstream, and business along with it, looked at the internet opportunity as a connectivity paradigm. It is there where coders and management often naturally disagreed or did not understand each other. Two paradigms were colliding. The challenge in this conversation is to understand where the real value was. Most people thought connectivity, and a few voices were telling the story of a deconstructed, agile, and exponential opportunity.

Coders were the first to become creatively and strategically enabled. If three people can build and scale what big established companies did at the same time, like selling books or helping people with any question you would usually need a thousand people to answer, what else was possible?

After a century of deskilling and removing theoretical and business thinking from every worker, suddenly a few people could achieve things a company of thousands had once been needed to do. So the market first did what it had been doing for decades. It connected new specialist silos to its existing business structure and acquired specialist companies—a vertical approach to a horizontal problem.

This was the mindset and era that created "Flash intros" on websites that no one wanted. It is probably the reason at least a third of all dotcom companies went bust. It is the reason why some startup ideas were hair-raising at best and lacked a sense of reality, yet were still getting funded.

Yes, the internet made us very connected, but we were connected before, weren't we? Isn't the real change the way we deconstructed every part of our life? The way we talk in 280 characters . . . how did that happen? The way we stay with strangers in their homes anywhere in the world. The way we know the name of our driver as if we had a chauffeur. The way we can work anytime and anywhere we like. The way we distribute a single conversation over five different apps. The way we deconstructed our attention into small consumable doses; the way new teams work, at work, iteratively. The way we stopped using our landline. The way even doorbells feel outdated: I'd rather call you than remember which doorbell I need to press because no one puts their name on them anymore.

If in business, we now talk about DevOps (development operations), DesignOps (design operations), or ResOps (research operations), we are talking about the same deconstructed systems now making their way into every other aspect of an organization. It is not just the customer side working along this principle. The differentator will be as Rachel Higham says: " . . . how you orchestrate the components together."

It is deconstruction that made the difference, not a constant increase in complexity. It set the stage for the necessity of wicked problem solvers.

# SEAN PARKER IS THE DEVIL

Sean Parker represents a particular time in the evolution of internet companies. Napster, Plaxo, and Facebook represent a threshold when a deconstructive mindset impacted the mainstream. Based on interviews and his work, I consider that Sean Parker had this mindset. Arguably, Zuckerberg did not.

Napster deconstructed the music album. It acted illegally for a while, but it showed what systems design, and embracing the deconstruction paradigm, can achieve. It was an object-oriented approach to the music album.

What should be mentioned is that back then, network speeds were reasonably low. There was a necessity to break things down into more digestible or transferable chunks. One advance was the Fraunhofer Institute's invention of MP3 as compression for audio files, which achieved an average of 75 to 95 percent reduction of file size. Because of the initial understanding of packages, one might consider that breaking up albums into single songs would be a sustainable or obvious way to create a system that could move songs and albums across the network. When music started turning into files, a coder's mindset would see different opportunities.

In this way, Sean likely combined two aspects of the equation: liking music and understanding deconstruction. Who doesn't like music? People had collected records and given each other mixtapes for a long time. In particular, creating a mixtape—using audio cassettes during the 1980s to create personalized lists of favorite music—and giving them to friends and loved ones was as illegal as Napster, in much the same way. Yet mixtapes were widespread and inspired the vibrant art form of sampling. Maybe the music industry at the time felt that mixtapes weren't as big a problem.

Music unites the world, and Napster united music lovers around the world to provide and share their music. When I first discovered it, the sheer amount of choice was flattening. The ease of use and power of a few thousand people sharing all their music was something with which no music store could compete. Early on, many bootlegs were shared: underground or amateur recordings of gigs with high value among fans. Because bootlegs[24] only had amateur distribution, the smallish community struggled to share hard copies of the music they loved. Using the internet to connect fans was a significant improvement: Napster made music easy to share around the globe. It also showed the speed with which a deconstructed system could snowball. With little to no marketing, it grew to 80 million users at its peak.

Napster was a significant disruptor to the content silos of record labels and distributors. In today's world, the record labels would have probably bought Napster's technology. Back in those days, the threat was so extraordinary to companies that no one had time to think about just buying them. The mindset did not exist in the industry. It would take Apple, a company that had never dealt with content, to embrace this opportunity and make billions where others were only litigating. In 2000, acquiring an internet company was not the usual thing to do, especially if it was challenging existing industries. Internet companies did internet things. Industry silos were safe. The paradigm gap between tools and world was so big that even artists did not understand the opportunity of having a distribution system, a straight line to their fans without the need for record labels. Napster had just deconstructed the relationship between artist and fan. It had shown record labels and distributors that they might not be needed anymore.

Deconstruction by definition removes obsolete parts. The middlemen are getting automated. You could say that they get enabled by new tools, but no one would look at it that way back then. Subconsciously deconstructing the way music could be distributed and added to the distribution network, Napster had created the future of music promotion, but no one lined up to buy it and use it, because the old paradigm needed a closed-up silo system, and Napster, based on OOP and deconstructive thinking, did not fall in line with this.

Eventually, Napster, Sean Parker, and Shawn Fanning had to close down the company. Sometime later, Apple managed to use its influence to establish iTunes as a centralized version of a deconstructed single song market. It looked the same on the surface, and Apple made a fortune from it.

Some time later, a university website built by a student coder named Mark Zuckerberg, who had used an idea from the now-famous Winklevoss twins, caught Sean Parker's attention. I am wondering, if Sean Parker saw the deconstructive characteristic of Facebook, or if he only had previous experience with platforms that looked like they could grow and thought this could be replicated.

Whatever articles or movies tell us at this point, Sean Parker saw some potential in Facebook. He got Peter Thiel involved and helped Mark Zuckerberg join the big leagues. Sean was the driver. Facebook likely exists because of his ability to see its potential and had previous connections. Remember there were many other social networks already—Friendster, Orkut, Myspace, and others. Parker was the perfect person to meet at that time. He had not only a new mindset but experience building an early tool and getting world feedback for something like this.

In many ways, Facebook started wicked, then used the tame model of fairly traditional online advertising as revenue. It struggled when trying to go mobile or break into VR. It is hard to tell how much Facebook has lost its wicked status once it just kept growing in size, or how much it has lost of its original ambitions.

For many, Sean Parker is still the devil, but not because of Napster's illegality or Facebook's aggressiveness ownership and growth. He was one of the first mainstream manifestations of a deconstructive or wicked mindset. Consciously or not, he jarred the existing paradigm. To the media, this made him one of the internet's early fallen angels, or if you will, a devil. He did not just collide with old paradigms but created tools that would further evolve and be even more misunderstood. Plaxo, one of his later endeavors, in a way was a better and more simplistic Facebook. Its focus was decentralized contact sharing—a purer idea that some people are still trying to recreate with blockchain and other technology decades later.

Napster was an elementary, deconstructed idea. It worked so well because it embraced a deconstructive mindset and the tools that came with it. It challenged the entertainment industry and showed many wicked characteristics by redistributing governance and enabling through tools. It is the first of many examples we should look back at, not for the way it challenged legal silos, but for the way it reduced friction and enabled a few people to do what usually needed extensive ecosystems.

# PIRATE BAY, THE MOST AWESOME CANCER

ew internet innovations have been more notorious and resilient than the Pirate Bay. It is one of the great examples of a tool created by the new mindset in its purest form. The establishment can only play cat and mouse with a platform that outperforms most legally established services. The gap between tame and wicked is so large that no one has even considered using what is right about the Pirate Bay for their business efforts.

Pirate Bay's underlying technology BitTorrent is a deconstructed solution that represents a further cycle beyond what the internet achieved. For those who are unfamiliar with BitTorrent and the Pirate Bay, here is a simplistic explanation. When you use your browser to access a website, you are using an address like www.xxxxx.com to tell the browser what content to look for. The browser then goes to an internet address book, looks up the right server, and goes there to find the content you are seeking. Then it delivers a file like index. html or index.php to start creating your browser content experience. This is how Facebook, YouTube, Google, or any other website work. Sites like this tend to have issues with larger files, especially video, which represents the largest type of data mainstream users are using.

Downloading on BitTorrent works similarly. First, you need an address for the file you want to download. The difference is that you go to the Pirate Bay to look for the file's address. Pirate Bay and all

BitTorrent sites are nothing more than address books for files. The files themselves are not located on Pirate Bay or any other BitTorrent site servers. The address you are getting on the sites is a list of places where you can find some or all pieces of the file you are looking for. This is what the magic of BitTorrent is all about.

In a standard browser or "web client," a file only exists on one server. On BitTorrent, you will get the addresses of everyone that has the file or parts of it sitting on their servers. Where websites have a web client or browser to display data/sites, BitTorrent has a BitTorrent client that downloads pieces of files for you. This multiplies the amount of bandwidth available to get a file onto your system. Demand for files like *Game of Thrones* episodes or the latest and popular movies can be high. This means many people have the files on their systems. The more who have parts of the data, the more you can download it from simultaneously. When you use YouTube or Netflix, you download from one server. With BitTorrent, you download from hundreds of servers at once. This is why BitTorrent can download an HD movie in five minutes.

The convenience of having HD and Blu-Ray quality movies on your laptop, within a handful of minutes, is one of the reasons Pirate Bay is still relatively famous and highly competitive with any streaming service available. It has higher speeds, has a bigger library of content, is more sustainably scalable, and has been around a lot longer than Netflix.

Companies like Netflix would not be profitable if they were paying for thousands of machines, which they would need to accomplish the same speed across their service. BitTorrent has solved the issue of transfer speed elegantly by becoming faster the more users it has, not slower. It is the old SETI screensaver applied to file sharing.

BitTorrent has gone beyond Napster. It is deconstructed, and within it is deconstructed again, which makes its potential exponential.

The internet deconstructs a single message into many packages that would eventually arrive on a server individually, but BitTorrent goes one step further. It draws the pieces that need to be delivered from multiple servers, because it knows where duplications of this file exist. This lets it sometimes transfer parts of the same data from hundreds of sources. What this means is that it reacts correctly during high demand times. On other systems, the same file being requested hundreds of times slows down what a centralized server can deliver, but that makes BitTorrent faster.

If you have ever been at an open-air festival and tried to call a friend, you may have been exposed to the shutdown of a nearby cell tower, a centralized and tame approach to a network problem. Those towers have bottlenecks. If a few thousand people are trying to make a phone call at the same time, the tower reaches its cap and will stop delivering its service. Most traditional networks are built like that. Newer deconstructed tools and thinking can scale beyond that.

The Pirate Bay has been up and down, hit by lawsuits and blocked, only to come back within 24 hours. Its resilience has not been matched by any other internet service except, perhaps, WikiLeaks. Since its inception, the Pirate Bay has cloned itself and now exists as many proxies or copies of the same site. If one site was hard to shut down, now it has truly become a hydra.

The internet has been exponentially growing. Networks or deconstructed systems tend to have exponential characteristics, which makes them very sustainable. The trouble is that most modern tools have still been held back by the siloed thinking of the Industrial Revolution's business models and consumer experiences. It is not enough that the tools have the potential. Mindset and world need to align for success. What remains is the question of why neither Napster nor BitTorrent's technology was picked up and used for modern commercial services. Both models are enormous steps toward zero friction. Regardless of how great the tool is, if the mindset or world feedback is not aligned, the tool doesn't succeed the way it should.

At some point, Pirate Bay founder Peter Sunde admitted that with all the clones out there, even he doesn't know where the Pirate

Bay exists anymore. It had become a viruslike entity that moved from server to server, and it could, because it was deconstructed enough to become an integral part of the internet. Convicting the founders of aiding copyright infringement feels meaningless if you know that they have little to do with the platform at that point. When a tool becomes so deconstructed that individuals don't matter anymore, it has reached a low effort of maintenance and a high level of production. It becomes somewhat like an idea you can't kill anymore.

It is easy to see how new wicked thinking can clash with a siloed business model. If the way you are making money is through controlling access to a product or resource, how would a system that freely and frictionlessly moves that product or resource align to your business model? It wouldn't, and that is why many companies should look at changing their business model. Google and Facebook represent search and content. Are they making money with those products? No. They make money with the advertising associated with them. That is a one-step-removed approach to making money—a deconstructed way of making money.

Earlier, I called Pirate Bay a cancer of the internet. These new systems share many characteristics with cancer or viruses. They are cheaper, quicker, and easier to scale. The more you deconstruct, the more opportunities you attract. The big difference is that tame thinking keeps you trying to make money out of the thing you build. Wicked thinking makes money out of the thing that others create with their energy, on top of what you build. If the internet was level one, Napster and BitTorrent were level two and three.

# POPCORN TIME

Imagine the download speed and ease-of-use of Pirate Bay combined with the movie data from IMDB.com combined with the look of Netflix, but even more user-friendly. This was Popcorn Time.[25] Like many other great projects, Popcorn Time was put together to test what a free, deconstructed streaming app that didn't have the usual siloed restrictions would look like.

The Argentinian creators argued that uneven distribution of movies and content did not make much sense to them in the age of the internet. Films like *There's Something About Mary* only appeared in South America years after its initial release in the U.S. Siloed content hindered commerce and accessibility where there was a market that would want access to the content at the same time as the rest of the world.

Popcorn Time combined multiple torrent tracking sites, resources of file locations with IMDB.com—the internet's most extensive database on movie and TV data. This meant that any file listed in the app had all content descriptions, actor lists, and review information automatically added to it. The app likely represented the internet's biggest library of entertainment content, something Netflix or Apple's iTunes would find hard to match.

In contrast, established companies like Samsung have tried to make their TV experience smarter but have not opened their product to deconstructed thinking. In an age where Google delivers anything people enter into its search field, they—and most likely other makers—are stuck with siloed channels or content resources far away from the zero-friction world consumers anticipate. Apps like YouTube or Hulu are treated like individual channels, and the TVs are overloaded with an app for every "channel." Even Amazon does not differ between its book and movie offerings. It is a single search for a whole catalogue. In 2004, Apple introduced Spotlight, its new search feature which could look on your laptop and the internet and even inside PDFs and other text files to find what the user was looking for.

A few years ago, I was helping create a new type of interface for one of Samsung's smart TVs. The team's ideas were quickly going "too far" for Samsung, because of the way the company was locked into contractual and other content silos to provide a more contemporary TV experience.

Mashups were all the rage some years ago. A mashup is a synergetic combination of two or more services or data sources. The very reasons data sources can be connected is because they have been deconstructed before. This lets other people reorganize a group of sources and services and create meta-services bigger than the individual parts, creating additional value that can be sustainable and have a business case.

This is what Popcorn Time did, and if it had not felt the pressure from siloed businesses, it could have easily challenged any of the big content providers. Again, someone should have bought it.

BitTorrent and Pirate Bay have been locked into the piracy and copyright infringement narrative. They are perceived as tainted goods, so no one commercializes this deconstructive tool, despite the competitive edge it can create. We needed the technology to come back from hiding under a new name, called blockchain, to be reconsidered as an opportunity. Yes, blockchain and BitTorrent are sisters. They are just variations of each other. The world is not that complicated and overwhelming after all, is it?

The line of illegality is often temporary. For example, up until some time ago, companies would not be able to patent life. Then genes of DNA like BRCA1 and BRCA2—or, in more straightforward language, the genes identified as responsible for breast cancer—were patented by a company called Myriad Genetics. A few years later, the U.S. Supreme Court decided that one can't patent genes. Similar things happened around cryptocurrencies. Pirate Bay and BitTorrent technology are still considered bad technologies. Time to look back at how we could enable people with some of those tools. Time to evolve that mindset.

# ILLEGAL! THIS TIME: BITCOIN

New ideas tend to challenge the status quo. Wicked ideas have a higher tendency to do so and are often considered illegal because they collide with mindsets that are tame by nature. From team silos to business models, everything needs to be upgraded. This change sounds threatening, and the primary reaction is often to reject and take legal action instead of integrating.

Bitcoin is based on blockchain. Blockchain and BitTorrent are very similar in the way they use deconstructive thinking to solve a problem. BitTorrent stores and accesses data, or parts of it, from multiple servers to fulfill a request for a user who wants to download a file. Blockchain stores identical and complete files or data entries on several servers to compare the exact copies for possible tampering with the data. Where BitTorrent uses the deconstruction to increase access and availability, and therefore speed, to its service, blockchain reduces the ability to tamper with existing data by storing exact copies in multiple locations.

It requires a network of computers to help manage all data, to keep the records of the blockchain ledger up to date. In 2008, a person calling himself Satoshi Nakamoto was identified as having created Bitcoin, a digital currency based on a blockchain to manage the currency transactions. One of the exciting aspects of Bitcoin was, and is, that there are a limited number of Bitcoins. What happens when more value enters the currency is that Bitcoins get atomized more and more into smaller and smaller fractions.

When Bitcoin first arrived, few took notice. Something wholly virtual and crypto-complicated was hard to identify as an opportunity. Further deconstructing the system, people could help Bitcoin by helping manage the transactions. Just as in blockchain, a network of computers helps calculate the transactions or data movements. Bitcoin added another incentive to the mix. To attract people, and their computers, to help calculate the transaction, Bitcoin introduced "mining," which means every helping computer got paid in Bitcoin for the contribution to the system.

Deconstructed thinking had a significant impact on redefining the roles of how people, and other parts of the system, engaged with a system and contributed to it. The Industrial Revolution had a more straightforward, explicit understanding of who contributed and for whom the system was produced. Ideators, producers, and consumers of the system's creations were demarcated roles. The new paradigm has introduced more flexible roles and therefore a different set of people who ideate, produce, and consume any service or product. Sometimes these roles are contextual, and one person can have multiple roles depending on context.

Modern systems are often not centralized, because centralized governance would create unsustainable friction or would not be economically feasible. The ambition to shut down Pirate Bay is a good example where multiple centralized control entities have tried to control the platform, but have continuously failed. The recent news of Facebook failing to identify malicious content that influenced the U.S. elections among its billions of messages is another example of a tame approach failing to solving a wicked problem. This failure does not prove that Facebook could not find a solution, but the default attempt to use tame mechanics like blocking and legal action is futile from the start.

Deconstructed content platforms like Facebook, YouTube, Wikipedia, and Twitter have, for a long time, run on the 90/9/1 rule or principle. The numbers might not be as conveniently cut in reality, but the point is that these three numbers represent the engagement levels or distribution of users on a given platform. It means only about one percent of users are creators of content for the platform. Nine percent are contributors, who do not create content but edit and modify, which means anything from resharing to commenting to editing and expanding existing content. Ninety percent are lurkers, the majority who consume and never contribute. Facebook still has 510,000 comments and 136,000 photos posted per minute. It needs solutions on an exponential complexity level to approach this kind of problem.

We are redefining the simple roles of producer and consumer and replacing them with a more complex or organic alternative. Bitcoin, not unlike Napster and the Pirate Bay, had shifted the content production and distribution to its users. Producer, distributor, and consumer can be the same person.

Who contributes how and who holds value where is shifting. Bitcoin was first traded as a currency. This gave legislators a challenge: was it a currency or not? For some time, it existed in legal limbo because what its value represented did not align with current rules and mindsets. Also, it was used to trade on a digital marketplace called Silk Road, and Silk Road was very illegal. It sold credit card numbers, drugs, guns, and even assassination contracts. The site was eventually shut down by the FBI in 2013, but Bitcoin was tainted as the currency of illegal online trade. For a short period, a new regulation made the trading of Bitcoin illegal, which crashed or closed down most Bitcoin trading platforms. The law existed only for a short time as regulators reversed their decision and Bitcoin could then be legally traded. This is documented in the documentary *The Rise and Rise of Bitcoin.*[26]

As a currency, Bitcoin is becoming part of the financial industry.

It can be used online and in some real-world shops. It offers many benefits like privacy, security, and a very low cost in a transaction. Though it has escaped its illegality phase, it is still heavily scrutinized. However, its history has inspired imitators.

ICOs (initial coin offerings) are a way to start a new cryptocurrency like Bitcoin. There is no real cost to back up new cryptocurrencies, which means everyone can give it a try to attract attention and, for a time, a value increase can make some money for a few. Some ICOs have attracted millions of dollars, which means some people have invested a lot of money into these new deconstructed versions of currency to gamble for a quick value increase. This gambling has misdirected attention away from the real value of cryptocurrencies: more frictionless transactions. At the time I am writing this, ICOs have become such a misunderstood and overhyped new piece of technology that Burger King launched an ICO in Russia and rap artist Ghostface Killah is launching a crypto-launch company. Cryptocurrency and the blockchain have come from illegality to short-term gamble. In an era where investment bots are starting to make a real impact, it is fascinating to see such technologies going through different phases of acceptance.

In a post-economic crash era, deconstructed systems, if not better understood, can both elevate and wreak havoc on our already shifting values and global situation. The tame approach of making a quick buck conventionally creates a questionable narrative.

The security and low cost of a transaction and the fact that no central entity controls such a currency, is a great opportunity. For a long time, countries have tried to get rid of central banks. Crypto might offer a new way out of our existing credit cycle. On the other hand, these currencies provide a method of turning more significant assets into investment opportunities the size of sand particles. Depending on what is backing the value of the currency, you can break huge assets into the tiniest bits and make investments available in many new ways to many new people.

Many inventions have collided with the law in ways apparent at the time of invention. Zuckerberg got told off for illegally scraping every student record off the university website to feed his first projects. Now Facebook is being investigated for letting Russia influence the U.S. election. Galileo Galilei had to spend his life under house arrest for his idea that the sun is the center of our solar system. The inventor of the electrical pylon tower was nearly killed by a mob. Jesus was crucified, Mandela was imprisoned. Larry Flynt was sued more times than it was probably worth. Martin Luther King Jr. was beaten up and eventually shot. Elon Musk wasn't allowed to sell his cars online in some U.S. states; the only alternative would have been for him to build a "brick and mortar" car sale. Steve Jobs' early business partner, Steve Wozniak, the true genius behind Apple's first products, was a phone freak and built a little electronic device that imitated old digital phone switchboards. With this device, one could make free phone calls, but it was one of the early examples of hacking and therefore illegal. Hackers themselves were, for a long time, chased by the law, even though their main aim was to point out security flaws in early company networks. Many ended up working for the companies they hacked as security specialists.

Today, Uber is causing a stir in many countries because it tries to circumvent the old legislation of the cab industry. In countries like Colombia, the app is illegal, but there are still Uber drivers and riders. Healthcare is so guarded by legislation and approvals, which are tied to exorbitant amounts of money, that only the big healthcare and pharma companies can afford to put a product to market. It is likely that wicked startups will hit this industry and clash with it legally. We can expect more such stories. Deconstructed mindsets and tools are bound to conflict with the old system. It does not mean that the tools are illegal. It means that the value and purpose are not aligned with the previous mindset. Once they are, rules will be adjusted, and new values will be accepted and integrated.

Consider this story:

A lovely little girl was holding two apples with both hands. Her mum came in and softly asked her little daughter with a smile, "My sweetie, could you give your mum one of your two apples?"

The girl looked up at her mum for some seconds, then she suddenly took a quick bite on one apple, and then quickly on the other.

The mum felt the smile on her face freeze. She tried hard not to reveal her disappointment.

Then the little girl handed one of her bitten apples to her mum and said, "Mummy, here you are. This is the sweeter one."

Especially when we face a new mindset in a new world, an open approach might help us see value and opportunity in what seems destructive or illegal.

Napster, Amazon, Facebook, Uber, and Airbnb are all symptoms of wicked thinking applied to different contexts. They all use the same recipe. You don't need to be a coder to be able to understand how to look at these things. Break reality down into logical parts as much as the deconstructive tools allow. I hope that at this point you can see that these deconstructive tools, even though they have popped up in different industries, are just an evolution of the same idea in different areas and contexts and therefore have different names. In part three, I will elaborate on how you can take your steps to create the same kind of wicked ideas.

As I am writing this, Facebook just announced their own cryptocurrency called Libra. For a company still showing many tame characteristics and having recently faced many wicked problems it is still failing to solve, it is a very interesting move for them to take on more of the same. I would like to say that it shows how something new can become openly adopted after a phase of clashing with old rules, but so far the launch of the currency has only led to calls for appropriate legislation that controls Facebook's new attempt at making more profit.

## IFTTT, TWILIO, AND THE APIS

APIs are beautiful examples of tools that enable wicked ideas. Imagine a LEGO set where other people come up with their own LEGO pieces. Companies like Google, Twilio, or IFTTT have based their business models on these new types of deconstructed products, and Jeff Bezos once wrote an infamous memo that his company would essentially fire every employee who did not embrace APIs in all of their internal day-to-day business. APIs are the most potent example of tools to enable the wicked mindset and get ideas into that exponential opportunity space. They have allowed us to create a world with wicked solutions faster and more iteratively.

APIs, or application programming interfaces, are a bit of a mixed breed. They look like silos of controlled access, but they represent deconstructed entities to put solutions in hyperdrive. Imagine a defined service, like a phone booth or a hot dog stand. Both objects have very controlled access points and a small handful of options and functions. They are, in theory, capable of doing more, but their service has been limited to a few clearly defined interactions with their surroundings.

A phone call in a phone booth needs to be paid for in a certain way, and the number is entered in a certain way. It does not have your address book on it, and you can't run internet data services through it, even though the line would be able to carry it, theoretically. All you can do is make a phone call.

The hot dog stand is similar. All you will get from it is a hot dog. You have to talk to the salesman to get the hot dog; you can't make the hot dog yourself. But you are given options: onions or no onions, ketchup or no ketchup, mustard or no mustard.

APIs are quite like that. You have a set of services, and they are somewhat restricted but flexible enough to cover most requirements. APIs have the biggest power when they are public, which means that they are accessible on the internet for everyone to use effortlessly.

This means a phone booth for everyone on the planet whenever they need one. Yes, I just described a mobile phone, only without the same price tag. Or imagine a hot dog stand that would pop up wherever and whenever you would need one.

Remember the objects from OOP. APIs are groups of objects neatly packaged up for everyone to use. Where Napster and Pirate Bay deconstructed files for people to listen to music and watch movies, APIs have done so with software services and code capabilities. Straightforwardly and compellingly, these micro-services—if we want to call them that—have allowed us to build amazing solutions on top of their capabilities. This structure has created exponential opportunities for Amazon and Google and many smaller companies because APIs are so easy to produce. This ease of production has also created more wicked problems and solutions because the solutions built with them evolve and the APIs underneath evolve as well. This is true for many services you are using. They have become continuously changing systems.

Google, Stripe, Twilio, IFTTT and other companies do so well because making APIs and their value available to the world is at the core of their business model. They enable wicked solutions.

ProgrammableWeb[27] identified the power of APIs a long time ago. At the time of writing, it tracks and writes about over 19,000 APIs, the business value they are creating and the opportunities they represent. It covers APIs in over 300 categories, such as accessibility and accounting to wine, word processing, and ZIP codes. ProgrammableWeb has been tracking since 2005. From 2017 to 2018 alone, about 2,000 APIs have been added. Not using or producing APIs is an immense value lost and trick missed.

Every single API represents a team of people taking care of a particular functionality that your business could provide. They do this for a fraction of the cost, which includes maintenance and constant improvement. All these are reasons why startups can develop very functional and fast prototypes of their services in very little time. For example, I used Stripe to help a startup enable card payments in just a few hours. This does not mean, however, that startups are merely copying other people's work. When you want to build something, you wouldn't make a hammer; you would buy one. On Spotify, you do not buy the album to listen to the song—you look for it and play it.

We live in a service and experience economy. Goods and products have become commodities. They do not represent the differentiating value anymore. We have moved on to more complex solutions tackling more wicked problems. If you are a modern company, your value will likely be in the particular way you are combining and using a hundred different puzzle pieces. Your competition might use AR or social media, but only you will be using it in a way that makes you stand out. If a twelve-year-old can set up a server and use the same API services your engineering team is using, what sets you apart? It will likely be the way you handle things, the way your team works together in your company, and the way you engage with your context of customers and partners.

In 2011, after Jeff Bezos had watched a talk by Google—which at the time had already embraced an API and deconstructive approach to their business—he released a famous internal memo, which leaked due to its "straightforwardness." Having seen that Google turned any new internal tool into a publicly accessible and commercialized product, he wrote:

1. *All teams will henceforth expose their data and functionality through service interfaces.*
2. *Teams must communicate with each other through these interfaces.*
3. *There will be no other form of inter-process communication allowed: no direct linking, no direct reads of another team's data store, no shared memory model, no backdoors whatsoever. The only communication allowed is via service interface calls over the network.*

4.  *It doesn't matter what technology they use. HTTP, Corba, Pubsub, custom protocols don't matter.*
5.  *All service interfaces, without exception, must be designed from the ground up, to be externalizable. That is to say, the team must plan and design to be able to expose the interface to developers in the outside world. No exceptions.*
6.  *Anyone who doesn't do this will be fired.*
7.  *Thank you; have a nice day!*

In simple terms, Bezos realized that any internally produced tool or service should be made available as a product to monetize, and why not? Companies should use what they think works best. That includes their products. It is necessary that every tool that your company is using should be able to be used by customers or clients out there. You could argue that this is the entrepreneurial spirit, but it is also confidence in what your company produces. Now that tools can reach billions, companies can grow fast and sustainably through people enabled by a smart combination of tools. The least one can do is consider if any business processes you have and could automate are automated or expanded as API-driven modules to improve operations and free up time for wicked opportunities.

Consider Twilio. Twilio creates automated phone boxes online. They are the computerized voices you hear when calling up a robot customer service. Most of their services need to be bespoke, so they turned their service into an API and let developers and producers on the client side create solutions without any need to consult Twilio.

Where traditional business growth approaches look for a big client first, Twilio's founders wanted to go grassroots. It made sense to get quality approval from the people who produced the solution. They were the ones who would find and test your service. They would tell procurement. It is not a top-down investment. Developers will dig in and analyze what your service can offer. Twilio went straight to the people who would engage with their offer. They deconstructed the customer relationship and business growth process. Going to a senior contact of a large business to make 1,000 unit sales is a tame approach, and being able to convince twenty people at a corporation that your service rocks can be a hard pitch. Every person will have different requirements for their departments and projects.

Over nine years, more than twenty angel investors and VCs told Twilio's founders that focusing on developers was the wrong strategy. But the developer-focused approach paid off big time when Jared Hecht and Steve Martocci used Twilio's SMS API to prototype a group messaging app during the TechCrunch Disrupt New York hackathon that Twilio sponsored in 2010. The app was called GroupMe, which went on to raise $11.45 million and became Twilio's single largest customer at the time by far. The company acquired over 28,000 paying customers, raised $233.7 million in venture capital, and launched a nearly $2 billion IPO on the New York Stock Exchange.

Going out wicked pays back wicked, and running an API-based business is different because as a service, it behaves like a network node, not like a single serving for a single customer. Scanning the exponential opportunity network that your idea is connected to costs time and money. A public API can provide you with organic lead generation that was previously just not possible. In an era where product launches can be so agile that they might pivot a few weeks into being live, being able to try many things in a short amount of time has become an acceleration factor. If a thousand potential customers can do that for you, without having to talk to your sales department, no investor will complain.

The approach to the customer has been de-siloed and reversed. Now the customer can check your offer out at their leisure. The old methods are not wrong, but they can't scale in a wicked world. Where previously only a handful of ways existed to start a relationship, today's many entry points, automated or not, have created a much larger number of ways to grow a business. A wicked company can deconstruct its product or service and has a sales and growth strategy that aligns with it.

As Twilio founder Jeff Lawson says, "We on-board developers like consumers and let them spend like enterprises . . . "

Deconstructive models shift the role and governance of a service or offering. This is not losing control as a company to what someone else can do with your service. An API is still a very controlled and carefully designed access model. It hides your magic algorithm or any unique selling point within the black box of the API while exposing the value and power of your product. If you remember the mindset-tool-world cycle, it is essential to see that an API sits between tool and world to create synergistic feedback. This means you can collect live user data—both qualitative and quantitative—for which you would usually pay a lot of money.

For me as a designer, there is something beautiful about the structure of a company's API. It can reveal what a company is good at delivering and where it is struggling, and it can be a manifestation of its focus as. Being that close to your customers is a great benefit for faster success, and it is worth considering that the way you bring your APIs to the customer is part of your brand.

As Tim O'Reilly said, "A platform beats an application every time."

An API is a platform of sorts. Platforms can have multiple APIs. We think of them like LEGO pieces, and LEGO itself has used deconstruction very well. Its licensing approach to selling *Star Wars, Harry Potter,* and other franchises in block-versions shows a tame company becoming wicked. It applies more complexity to its offerings, moving from selling plastic blocks as a product to the experience of being able to create any story there is. LEGO has gone on to make computer games—online tools with virtual bricks, referencing very successful movies. It stands out as an example of what can be done when you deconstruct your offer and let your customers give you better ideas on what to do with your product.

The forecast and validation of the API based market are significant. Mindcast projects that the telecom API market alone will grow to over $200 billion in revenue in the next three years. My last project was at a telco, and we turned their IT essentially into the same deconstructed and interdependent shop that can grow and scale through the same API-like mechanisms.

APIs are wicked tools. They let you scale exponentially and establish your offer so close to your customers that the new variety and complexity of those relationships will feel not daunting but reassuring. Consider everything you build and use to have the right kind of world feedback.

# DON'T GET ME STARTUPPED

Startups are not an indicator of innovation. They never were. People in a startup are not geniuses. All a startup represents is the long overdue format of an outcome-based team of cross-disciplinary people who can get to a solution of scale or benefit, faster. They achieve this with a deconstructive mindset and tools and a network of consumers and partners who think like that too. They are wicked teams, not genius teams. The problem is, not many startups are consciously deconstructed. Most only try to copy others.

The idea that startups are by default innovative looks dubious at best for people who have been working with technology since the dot-com boom. Facebook was not new; it existed as Friendster, Orkut, and Myspace already. Facebook got more money and attention than its predecessors, so it became more sustainable. Uber was not the first idea of its kind. Sidecar launched around the same time, and I used Hailo in London for quite a while before Uber was a thing. Pokémon GO, a GPS-based game, had dozens of noncommercial predecessors from various countries dating back to more than ten years before the game came out.

Facebook, Uber, and Pokémon GO do look innovative to tame companies and people with a tame mindset. That includes most journalists, and as a result, we have a very misleading narrative of why startups were a significant development.

## Young people are just smarter.

### —Mark Zuckerberg

The Zuck might have used some PR spin there, but as David Epstein quotes in his book *Range,*[28] a tech founder who is fifty years old is nearly twice as likely to start a blockbuster company as one who is thirty, and the thirty-year-old has a better shot than a twenty-year-old. We have to be more careful in separating myth from real-world data.

What startups have shown us is what your wicked teams should look like. Their level of self-governance, cross-disciplinary nature, and tools that let three people do the work of 300 is the significance.

For too long, companies have used tame tools and tame ways of working. While companies kept their outdated model of creating products and services, engineers realized that the new tools enabled them to produce faster and in smaller teams. It helped them to use their new mindset to create the deconstructed tools which they felt were better than those the companies were using.

It has been a big problem for siloed companies to build cross-disciplinary teams. Their processes have been optimized for a silo and waterfall approach. Even in teams with a more modern, agile approach, acceleration within a silo does not create the horizontal and deconstructed benefit that a startup team can offer.

A startup team can more easily look across a set of silos at the same time. Startup teams have reversed the deskilling culture first: team members in startups tend to own and contribute more than just one skill. I have seen many startups that are too tools-focused, but incubators and accelerators have uplifted capabilities more and more, so that even tech-focused startups can gather business and human-centered research skills needed to validate and grow their ideas.

Their setup is focused on a complete end-to-end solution and outcome. Research, business case, production, and day-to-day operations are all within this outcome package. Marketing and sales or pre-sales are naturally combined on platforms like Kickstarter or Product Hunt, all part of a vast deconstructed network of tools that act as anything from accounting to CRM to marketing functionality.

Kickstarter is seen as a funding platform, but it is more often used as a PR platform for products, and a price testing or proof of concept exercise opportunity. When I managed The Things Network's campaign, it was clear to see that the PR effect outperformed the revenue of the products. Data does not show a correlation between the amount raised on those platforms and the funding raised through VCs, but VCs are using those platforms for risk assessment. They have deconstructed the shopping experience: instead of buying from the factory outlet, one buys straight from the prototype lab. And they added a marketing and community building tool to it by creating a new type of customer relationship. The result of this tight product-to-customer chain builds so much trust and support from customers that I have seen people donating money to a Kickstarter campaign without expecting a product in return.

Since platforms like Kickstarter and incubators, accelerators, and VCs are all in place, startups have options on how to finance their effort. They are enabled, cross-skilled, business-strategy aware and have deconstructed financing. You should have teams like that at your company. In some of my projects, we called those teams *intrapreneurial.* Startup teams are not unique in being able to work like this—every company can have that kind of team—but in a wicked company, those wicked teams need a support system. Most of the times when even a great idea with lots of money failed, this support system was missing.

We should not look at startups for innovation. We should not look at startups for the place where true geniuses drink their matcha tea. We should look at startups for how to enable new teams and ways of working. The investment is lean and iterative. The risk is deconstructed by those investment and production cycles, and it can scale using the same approach.

In 2002, Google's chief economist, Hal Valerian, stated, "Maybe the internet's role is to provide the inexpensive communications that can support mega-corporations."[29]

My version of this statement would be "Maybe the deconstructive nature of tools like the internet enables us to create organizations that provide more value to society."

Fifty years ago, Warren Bennis had an idea about the shift in team and business structures: "What then will be the characteristics of a super-industrial society?"[30] He foresaw a future where problems would be solved by task forces composed of relative strangers who represented a set of professional skills and who gathered temporarily.

This was someone describing startups or deconstructed, cross-disciplinary teams half a century ago. Some ideas take a long time until they find the right context in which to grow. I believe this time is now.

Startups do not have to exist outside of larger companies. Could we imagine a company with a few thousand employees that are a community of temporary teams? Could a company exist similar to the Pirate Bay, Napster, or Bitcoin, where the deconstructed platform is the center and hundreds or thousands of small teams contribute to a more significant purpose and product or service? I am wondering how much open-source projects are like this or which of my previous examples could be closest to this idea. Could one rebuild companies like Procter & Gamble or British Telecom into such an entity? If we think of Napster and the Pirate Bay as networks with progressive nodes of individuals or enabled teams, how lean and efficient could a wicked company get?

When commentators say many modern companies have fewer employees, they forget that over a billion people produce Facebook and YouTube's content. An even more significant number of people tell Google's search engine and APIs every day what they are looking for and what they find relevant. This is where these companies got wicked. They shifted governance and production and turned it into temporary transactions. Google gives you a search result and gets your data as currency in exchange. Customers have also become content or data creators.

A *Fortune* article from 2017 calculated that the tech giants Apple, Facebook, and Alphabet (Google) had a worker value that outperformed the Detroit Three of Chrysler, Ford, and General Motors.[31] This is an apples (no pun intended) and oranges comparison. Making cars is still mainly a hardware type of business. Hardware is hard and costly—ask Elon Musk. Software costs are negligible when creating a thousand instances of the same product. Tesla is probably the most tech-driven car maker today, yet struggles to scale its production. Apple does make most of its money with hardware, but it is considered a luxury brand based on the margins for its phones. The car makers don't have the same margins, and Apple makes money with content and apps on top of that.

The bottom line is that wicked companies have wicked teams. They use deconstructed thinking and tools. They have flexible and evolving skills beyond role silos. They can self-organize and self-govern. They understand the purpose and ambition of the business. They have ideas on how to communicate the product and engage with their customers. This is why they can create exponentially more value than tame teams. Startups aren't smarter, but they have a more inclusive approach and a wicked, not tame, support system.

# WICKED IS HERE

In 1970, when Alvin Toffler wrote *Future Shock,* he saw the early shift in mindset away from the ideas of the Industrial Revolution. The shifts were significant enough for him to describe the change as a shock for society. He described temporary teams that worked remotely or in the absence of classic company constraints. He described service-based businesses and an atomization of people's activity in even smaller social groups. Around 1990, a new set of tools and ecosystem started to become economically relevant, and a gold rush made companies jump at anything considered connected. This created a set of tools that could build better solutions for complex or wicked problems. It was a natural progression; once we had mastered the fundamental challenge of mass production, society wanted to solve the next level of problems.

Advertising led the way by telling us that a product was not just functional, but offered a certain quality, an experience, a lifestyle. Then we started to be able to create those experiences not just for people with money, but for the mainstream. Many companies along the way made the mistake of hiring wicked people and teams only to create functional or tame new aspects of products and services. People do not want those anymore. What successful companies are showing us is that enabled, de-siloed teams with the right support can create wicked solutions that serve customers' needs and are more impactful against wicked problems. We can now find solutions for constantly evolving problems. This is where the new value lies.

As a company, you will want the mindset-tool-world cycle equally present. You will wish your designers and developers to think object-oriented or deconstructed, and you will want them supported by everything from money to business principles and communications activities.

In Part Three, I will go into more detail on how these aspects should work together and how to make your business more wicked.

This is
a Tame Problem.

This is a
Wicked Problem.

# PART III

# WICKED GAMES

**Thoughts and actions to become wicked.**

The Industrial Revolution introduced companies that can be described as tame companies because they solve tame problems very well. They tend to be deskilled, be heavily siloed, put a lot of value on specialists rather than generalists, and believe people need management to function.

We have established in part two that the mindset, the tools, and therefore the world have shifted and enable companies to solve wicked problems instead of tame problems. Wicked problems have a particular set of characteristics. People who want to create wicked solutions need to match those characteristics in the way they work and the information they use to identify the context of the problem and how to manifest a solution.

Through a wicked lens, most problems will look tame again.

# WHAT NOT TO DO

Wicked companies are built on three pillars: people first, tools last, and get to know the world as best as you can. Mindsets are within people, both employees and customers. This means change is within people, not tools. People make tools; they use tools flexibly and sometimes in unintended ways. People either adopt tools and services or don't. Whichever way you look at it, people are the driving force behind success or failure. Tools are enablers, and there are too many to count out there. Tools should enhance your current characteristics and ways of working. Forget about a cookie-cutter approach here. Pay attention to what tools a company embraces and avoids. It is a business decision if you do better with a Swiss Army knife or a katana sword. Embrace the world. It is a wicked place. It is easier than ever and more important than ever to know it well. This means constant learning is not an option but a necessity.

**If all you have is a hammer, everything looks like a nail.**

–Abraham Maslow, *The Psychology of Science*

Before I elaborate on some of the above in more detail, here is a short list of common fallacies I have been finding over the years. They seem to crop up a lot in tame companies and rarely show up in wicked companies.

## TOOLS LAST

Don't try to fix a business problem with a new tool. Tools are amazing enablers, but they are not silver bullets. Tools are highly contextual, which means the same tool can be either very good or very bad given its context. More progressive tools like Slack can be an improvement to using email, but it can be as messy and inefficient as email if people do not use it right. The biggest complaint about tools is that they are often dropped on teams without management having either consulted the teams or better understood the working context.

In a recent project, we were supposed to pick a code versioning tool for thousands of engineers in a large corporation. At the beginning of the project, someone mentioned that we are wasting our time researching the tool's context. "It is either GitHub or Subversion!" This was a very tame and tool-only focus approach to describe the problem and the solution. A quick round of human-centered research showed that the engineers, located across multiple countries and time zones, have country-specific tool preferences. Different countries use different tools, but projects did not reach outside of countries, so there was no tool conflict. Thousands of engineers using a tool that does nothing to help their performance made no sense at all. It would have been millions of investment dollars for no business benefit.

We pivoted the project and spent a lean budget on improving the use of the two tools respectively. This not only saved money but improved performance. If you work in a company with complaints about how bad the tools are, or a company where you can't find the functionality you need when you need it, you are too tool-focused. If you are missing the people and world aspect to solve your problems, then any investment you take will not give you the gain wicked companies get.

Do you have something like a tool master—a person who researches and collaboratively assesses and prototypes what tools to integrate and how to enable the workforce and its processes best? Are you only quantitatively doing this or creating valuable qualitative impact?

Procurement has a particular place in my heart. It does save money for the company in the short run, but I have seen much of those savings spent afterward for better tools or lost in lower efficiency of the process due to tools that were cheap but substandard. Does procurement need a more process- and human-centered, research-driven approach to assess costs and efficiencies?

New agile and iterative processes are getting faster every year. In the last ten years, I have not met a procurement process fast enough or fitting enough to provide the capabilities appropriately for any project. What could we do to improve this? I believe that we need a shift away from tools and toward what can help people work better.

## YOU GOT THE TALENT!

Progress and the risk of investment are kept alive by trust. The trust companies have in their workforce has been diminishing since the Industrial Revolution. Deskilling and silos have often led people across an organization to feel they cannot think for themselves, challenge the status quo, or get proactive around a problem or solution. This has not been on purpose, but by design. The increasing need for wickedness has led companies to hire specialists and acquire capabilities to improve their mindset. This communicates a lack of trust in existing employees' expertise and ability to learn. It is true that not everyone can adopt a new mindset. However, in my experience, a lot of potential is ignored when companies hire consultants or decide on risky acquisitions. Every company has people who go the extra mile and have skill sets that don't fit into the silo of their role. In one of my projects, we turned over 200 engineers into designers and analysts. We got 4,000 people aligned with our new process and approach.

You can buy yourself into a customer space, you can spend money on hackathons and acquiring specialist businesses, but the costs are a multiple of growing those capabilities yourself, and the friction will have you hemorrhage value. I have seen acquisitions work a bit, but I have also seen growth and trust in existing capabilities being ignored. If you can't grow yourself, you will keep spending multiples of what your competition does. It is worth creating a way to identify who can be part of your new wicked company. The trick is to look beyond silos and deskilling effects and rediscover who works for you. A Gallup poll from 2013[32] showed that only 13 percent of workers worldwide are engaged in their work and 24 percent are even actively disengaged. FastCompany reports that the average company loses 25 percent of productivity to drag or friction. Apple, Netflix, Google and Dell have 40 percent more productivity, but do not have significantly more talented employees. It is about what they do with the people they have. The obvious thing that stares one in the face is the potential that every organisation's people represent, but that is on average untapped.

On one of my previous projects, I led the creation of a center of excellence for British Telecom in the UK, BT Technology. To transform the company and its ways of working to modern standards, within a year we:

- created four evolving learning journeys to uplift capabilities across the business
- activated 5,500 design thinkers
- uplifted 200+ gold standard design thinkers who created outcome-based teams across the business
- mobilized twenty-eight IT services and project teams
- implemented a step-change cultural and digital transformation
- created significant business benefit through increased automation, reduced duplication, cost-savings and

identifying previously unknown problem areas and designing solutions for them

- started the future of work through creating teams that do operations, do design and are commercial thinkers all in one
- We did not hire new people to do so. All the new skillsets came from existing resources. All the project work was done by BT's own people, not trained consultants.

## DON'T LOOK AT THE SHINY LIGHT!

Jumping at trendy technologies and its features has been the sport of companies for a while now. At the time I am writing this, blockchain and the internet of things are high on the attention of investors. Novelty in tools has a magnetic effect, but in a world of black boxes doing complex algorithms, it is hard to tell which one will bring the next significant value. As I mentioned previously, people will make most of the difference. A lot of tech looks great, but people will not use it.

Troy Norcross of Blockchain Rookies, a specialist in all things blockchain, told me dozens of stories of companies that approached him only for him to ask why blockchain would need to be part of the solution proposed to begin with and not get an answer. The tool focus has become such a narrative for mainstream business that many innovations or investment efforts choose the novelty of the tool over the need of the world they are trying to turn into customers. Tools are tame things to measure. People and experiences are qualitative opportunities that only wicked companies measure.

Twenty years ago, when companies had just found out that e-commerce can sell products via a website, everyone needed one, fast. Anyone old enough might remember the infamous Flash intro for websites. It was an animated trailer or intro sequence that played full screen when anyone arrived at a company's website. Thousands were spent on a Flash intro. Two things happened relatively quickly after the intro was live on the site. First, a "skip intro" button was added as users complained about having to endure something that represented zero value to their shopping experience, not unlike the skip button on all contemporary YouTube ads. The second was that the intro was eventually taken down soon after it was put live. Experiencing it in situ and live convinced most people it was a hindrance rather than a benefit. Conferences were named after the infamous "skip intro" button. The technology of animation had been thought of as a value without any proof.

The investment money companies spend on the latest trend to be uncritically taken into consideration is a sign that the world and people are not investigated. Technology is a tool. Not every tool is right for your business. Not everyone will benefit from buying a chainsaw or a bread maker. New technologies are no different. They have to align with your company's mindset and behavioral context. The right technology will do well in your company if it is right for you. There are great ideas and innovations built on older technology: SMS to revolutionize patient relationships in healthcare, message boards and community platforms that engage their audience, simple stories that defy scientific mainstream by providing documentation for exceptions among parents with children on the spectrum. High tech is not better quality or innovation by default. The trend is instead that we will be more qualitative and people-focused, rather than building robots.

There is plenty of space to explore and validate as great opportunities. Funds and accelerators, unfortunately, put the focus on the latest tech. Do not be confused. Use the right tools because your customers or employees can create value with it. Ignore the shiny light.

## REALITY CHECK

It has never been easier to check with reality these days. Human-centered design, data tools, Google design sprints, rapid prototyping . . . it has never been cheaper and faster to check if an idea holds up in the real world. There is no excuse anymore for not knowing if a particular behavior or consumer need is not out there.

The phrase *eating your own dogfood* should be part of any company's vocabulary. What that means is that whatever you produce or offer, your organization should be using it, because they believe that it is worth using, because they have tested it themselves and know that it has purpose and value. This makes any person in the organization and its customers amazingly similar. We are living in the experience economy and people watch less advertising than ever. Whatever a company produces needs to hold up in reality, not in a made-up dreamworld of aspiration. In the age of polarized social media platforms, a small misalignment between reality and the authenticity of a brand can ruin your product. Consumers can smell nonsense quicker than ever, but they are welcoming everyone who engages and is authentic. This is both true internally and externally. When working on some transformation projects, that fact that teams were asked about their context and pains made some individuals write to their managing directors, thanking them for the fact that they were finally asked about how to improve their ways of working.

Reality exists both outside and inside your company. Both heavily contribute to your business's success. There is not enough money in the world to keep an idea alive that has no reality equivalent.

If only money made a difference, all the big companies would be the most innovative ones. But we intuitively know that isn't true. There have been too many cases where a small team looked at reality and found a great solution. There are too many cases where big companies spent a fortune having people sitting in a room coming up with ideas, disconnected from reality. A team of well-established and well-paid specialists were given the task of figuring out how to make man-made flight happen, but the Wright brothers built it in their garage on a shoestring budget.

## BEHAVIOR IS OR ISN'T

You can't create new behavior! Most new ideas will not surprise you, because they tend to align with existing behavior better than before. Some say that people didn't know they needed an iPhone or iPod. This only means people don't understand what those products brought to us. The iPhone made the internet usable on the phone! We loved the internet already by that point.

The same goes for social media. Why are people sharing their meals? People have shared their joys and frustrations for centuries. This is what social chatter is all about. Social media just let everyone do that in one global room. Uber was incremental. We needed cabs before. Now we get one by a click and know the driver's name in advance.

It gets trickier when you consider cultural context. QR codes were successful in Japan. Someone in the Western world saw them and was convinced that tools and behavior could easily translate beyond cultural context. Japanese phones came with a reader app installed, but in Europe, no one had one, so QR codes didn't take off outside of Japan. The infrastructure did not support the behavior. The lack of knowledge in the West did not encourage the behavior. Bluetooth beacons for retail failed in a similar matter. People generally don't like advertising, and they don't like keeping their Bluetooth switched on on their phone because it drains the battery.

The sharing economy is another example. Some people used to borrow a drill from a neighbor rather than buy or ever own one yourself. But in the age of Amazon, you can buy one for $10 and get it within an hour without the hassle to ask or care if your neighbor is at home or needs to use it when you would need it.

Tools and their trends are not a driver for consumers anymore. I can hardly tell if my new laptop processor is worth the money or makes my computer faster. I have no pixels visible on my screen anymore, so 4K means nothing to me. Game console wars based on performance are dead. It is all about the experience the console can deliver. VR is too cumbersome and expensive for us to consider it worth buying. I don't want any more devices I have to charge. Technology commoditizes too quickly. The trick is how and why you are using it, not what you use. A laptop doesn't make you a startup genius and a sportscar doesn't make you a rally winner.

# THE TWO TYPES OF SMART

**I have no special talent. I am only passionately curious.**

—Albert Einstein

O ur idea of specialists needs reconsidering. Humanity tends to lean toward the savior who singlehandedly saves the day. What if our new world requires a different kind of person—someone closer to a Renaissance person? Our world is complex and is getting more so every day. Are we missing a trick by expecting the genius to be our savior? Is it time for the polymath, the jack of all trades, to step into the foreground? The signs are there!

We like our knights in silver armor. Joseph Campbell's account of the Hero with a Thousand Faces shows our belief in a single savior throughout history. We tend to believe in our leaders, which is sometimes a blessing and has sometimes been a very, very bad idea. For some reason, we started to do the same with technology. Companies have blindly invested in new tech trends like social media, big data, VR, or Bitcoin. Many of them learned that it takes more than spending a lot of money and buying new shiny tools. Slowly, as technology has become more commodified, it has become more evident that it has always only been an enabler. As the world of big data says, "garbage in, garbage out": even the best algorithm or system can't produce gold if it only has bad or wrong data to work with.

Disciplines that help measure and design companies like to use the categories of people, tools, process, and information to find the right balance to uplift the capabilities of a company. We have seen that they can't predict change. Only recently have we started to move from quantitative to recognizing the qualitative value to be the driver for better positioning of a company. Qualitative value tends to sit across horizontal factors of an offering. It rarely aligns with a specialist silo.

I have been hired many times as a specialist or mad professor for a company that wanted change. Often, though, I was not allowed to connect the dots across silos. A single shiny skill was all that was expected from me. Without being allowed to combine this skill with others, I tried to bring together different skills as teams, often outside project parameters others had set. I was not alone. Around the time creative technology was a new type of role agencies would hire, I met dozens of people who had multiple skills but were not allowed to use them in their workplace. They were hired as and expected to be focused savants, single-silo mad professors with little to contribute to the process apart from trendy gimmicks, which most of them knew would have little impact for clients.

They were jacks of all trades, polymaths capable of bringing together a new way of working across silos. But they were not treated as such.

## A NEW SMART

The complexity of today's world requires multiple areas of expertise to work together to address any challenge. Startups and cross-functional teams have proven the success of this approach. They are the antithesis of the Industrial Revolution: they represent the mindset of a Leonardi da Vinci or any practitioner who would look at any area for inspiration. This is the deconstructed opportunity of the future.

The cross-disciplinary individual is not just a romantic notion. It has been scientifically proven that multiple skills within a person can have at least as much value for success as high-level specializations. Let me elaborate: According to Michael Simmons[33], there are two acknowledged paths to success for people:

1. **Genius:** Become the best at one specific thing.
2. **Polymath:** Become very good (top 25 percent) at two or more things.

Achieving and maintaining a genius level is very cost- and energy intensive. There is a reason it is lonely at the top: it requires exponentially more energy to stay ahead of the competition. Becoming a polymath requires a much lower level of energy and a different way of acquiring knowledge. It is easier to achieve. So it is expensive and inefficient trying to achieve value through the genius approach, especially in a deconstructed or horizontal context where polymaths can perform better.

Industries have lost money over the genius approach for some time. Like any other system, the higher within a vertical that you want to get, the exponentially larger the energy effort gets. I am not a quantum physicist, but I have seen game studios trying to live-scan every footballer's follicle to make a football game more realistic, and racing games recording car sounds in real-world contexts.

Titles like *Gran Turismo,* a racing game, push the design with each new release of the game to make the gaming experience more closely resemble reality through enhanced graphics, gameplay, and many other features. FIFA, the football/soccer game, invested heavily in 3D scanning the latest and most prominent players, spending a significant budget on licensing the use of their character and animating their famous moves and behaviors on the field in minute detail. The extra value for the gamer is small, but the company needs to up their "game" to justify the new release of the game, spending ever greater energy for less benefit.

The costs to make dust on the road authentic is enormous, and the added benefit to the gamer keeps getting smaller. It is like a professional athlete enhancing their body's performance. Diet, exercise, oxygen-deprivation simulations, high-oxygen infusions, and steroids are all high-cost efforts to stay at the very, very top.

Staying at the top twenty-five percent instead of the top one percent makes a huge difference. Furthermore, on the innovation side, the top one percent of siloed thinkers have run out of ideas, so should we still invest in geniuses?

Cross-disciplinary and entrepreneurial teams that work horizontally are only a transition phase.

As Tim Carmichael, ex-CDO of the British Army, told me, "We only ever approach problems horizontally today. Vertical does not work for us anymore."

Newer holistic practices like service design have collaboration and inclusion on the top of their list of principles. One way to read this is that they are on the right path to include new practices, thinking, and tools into their model. This is the progressive approach. This is a sustainable approach. These are steps toward a wicked level of being able to solve problems.

## GENIUS: THE DOWNSIDE

Many professions that started as deskilled jobs during the Industrial Revolution have evolved into specialized and niche silos. But they have run out of ideas because they only look at a very narrow part of the world. Their incentive is to stay within their niche because it positions them better. Scientists are a great example of a group of specialists that are more successful the more they get published. A published scientist is more likely to get funding or tenure. This leads to a very competitive field that locks up and fights over knowledge. A lot of energy is spent on staying at the top.

The Natural History Museum in London is a research facility as much as a museum. Working with scientists who have to fight with a first-to-market attitude was eye-opening to me. Keeping knowledge to yourself to be the first to publish has become a competition that is opposite to the collaborative and horizontal approach that most scientists would say their profession is about, but the system of siloed knowledge has created a market where it is more valuable not to share.

Chasing relevance in science has also created smaller and smaller silos of knowledge. Writing about the use of the comma in Shakespeare's works will look like a waste of energy for the uninitiated, but it might get you tenure. Modern problem solving is complex. Locking up knowledge and developing a language and ownership to maintain value artificially is counterproductive to progress. The commercialization of knowledge through copyrights and patents has furthered this hindrance of progress.

What has also evolved with specialist niches is a specialist language, yet another silo that makes working on complex projects in cross-disciplinary environments challenging. Time and money are spent on discussing which terminology, tools, and processes are more relevant, often to little benefit.

Real geniuses require a vast amount of energy, just like Olympic athletes, to stay on top or relevant. If we consider any effort of a company as an investment of energy, then geniuses require an enormous amount of energy to maintain. Einstein's famous theory of relativity states that systems balance themselves between the amount of energy used and benefit gained. As a *Guardian* journalist, Aloh Jha, describes:

> *Another feature that emerges from general relativity*
> *is that, as something speeds up, its mass increases*

*compared with its mass at rest, with the mass of the moving object determined by multiplying its rest mass by the Lorentz factor. This increase in relativistic mass makes every extra unit of energy you put into speeding up the object less effective at making it move faster.*

As the speed of the object increases and starts to reach significant fractions of the speed of light (c), the energy going into making the object more massive gets bigger and bigger.

Every system that is at the edge of its potential becomes more energy-intensive in this way. Current physics says that lightspeed can never be reached because the faster matter moves, the less efficient energy is at making it go faster. Nature has a habit of telling us our limits. Once that happens, we should look somewhere else. If we only know one thing, then it is very hard to move forward.

The world has heralded specialists for a long time as the primary drivers for progress. Many modern tools have commodified specialist skills, like building a website or tailoring a machine-learning system. What was previously only available to specialists is now readily available for or learned by generalists, polymaths, or T-shaped people in less time.

Twenty years ago, I had to learn about PIC chips and a good handful of hardware components to build my microcontroller, which I could only code into a PC. Today, I buy an Arduino from eBay for four pounds and plug it into anything. I like coding it with open source software.

Today, I don't have to know how to control a mainframe computer to create a service that reaches millions and changes the world. I don't have to be a genius anymore to build it. But I have to understand a combination of other aspects like marketing, psychology, business strategy, community management, and how to raise funding to make my idea a success because everybody else can build those things just like me.

Specialists are not useless, but they don't do well in a horizontal and collaborative world where multiple areas of expertise are needed to create a value that can grow. We need to consider that specialists are not always the answer. A siloed view does not do well in a wicked world.

As Daniel Epstein observes:

> *I dove into work showing that highly credentialed experts can become so narrow-minded that they actually get worse with experience even while becoming more confident--a dangerous combination. And was stunned when cognitive psychologists I spoke with led me to enormous and too often ignored body of work demonstrating that learning itself is best done slowly to accumulate lasting knowledge, even when that means performing poorly on tests of immediate progress. That is, the most effective learning looks inefficient; it looks like falling behind.*

It is not just the viewpoint that underdelivers. Imagine a team that needs to have many skills, one skill to one person. It would be big. If you instead have a team with cross-disciplinary people, it can be small and achieve the same outcome. Only looking at a small aspect of reality is not sustainable in a wicked company.

## "POLYMATH" IS A BAD WORD

When the new paradigm of tools and mindset hit industry after industry, companies continued to hire specialists to solve their problems. No one can be blamed for doing what had worked for decades.

Companies were naturally looking for specialists where they needed generalists. The generalists existed but either were not hired because they didn't fit the pattern of a specialist, or were hired and put into a silo where the context didn't allow them to do their job. This sounds extreme, but I have seen this many times. Many friends of mine who just wanted to work at companies tell similar stories.

Around the time when advertising wanted creative technologists, a lot of us were hired. Most of us had an eclectic mix of skills; often technology and design, but with strategy, business, or other aspects thrown into the mix. This mix created a lot of confusion in the agencies who tried to hire us. One agency told me that they didn't know if I was a coder or a designer so they couldn't hire me. Instead of appreciating getting two for one, they got none.

Another friend of mine sat over a year in a one-person department that no one who sold projects to clients knew about. He was never made part of the pitch team because he was assumed not to know how to sell, so he left a very well-paid job because he felt useless and without purpose. Others fought for change, only to be ignored or mistreated because their value was just not understood.

A lot of money was invested without understanding the problem. Many of my friends left the industries they used to enjoy working in out of frustration, never to come back. In my opinion, we lost a generation of very talented people to an era of initial change, where neither side knew what to do.

This is slowly changing. Transformation projects are more and more focused on changing mindsets and creating a more cross-disciplinary approach to business challenges. The jack of all trades is gaining value.

Polymaths have proven themselves throughout history, but often have been mislabeled as geniuses, maintaining the more popular narrative.

In *Human Accomplishments*[34], his expansive book on innovators, Charles Murray lists Newton, Galileo, Aristotle, Kepler, Descartes, Huygens, Laplace, Faraday, Pasteur, Ptolemy, Hooke, Leibniz, Euler, Darwin, Maxwell, Ben Franklin, Thomas Edison, Leonardo da Vinci, and Marie Curie as generalists. Modern-day polymaths include Elon Musk, Steve Jobs, Richard Feynman, Bill Gates, Warren Buffett, Larry Page, and Jeff Bezos.

Michael Simmons, in his article on "Modern Polymaths," makes an elaborate case that polymaths have been contributors to society and the science around this fact is gaining recognition. He references Robert Root-Bernstein's research on the correlation between the number of interests someone develops and their likelihood of cultural impact. This impact is higher the more interests someone has. Unsurprisingly, someone who knows more across various contexts and scenarios appears to find more or alternative opportunities more accessible. In most companies I worked with, I saw people who did more than the scope of their role asked. Do you know your polymaths? Does your company?

**It's technology married with liberal arts, married with the humanities, that yields us the result that makes our heart sing.**

**–Steve Jobs**

Leonardo da Vinci mixed his colors and created new ways of casting horse statues. Gaudi had a famously close creative relationship with his ironmonger, which resulted in innovative steel gate structures and designs. Bringing different skills together or unlocking multiple skills in people always leads to synergy.

Advertising learned this fifty years ago but may have forgotten since. Back then, art directors and copywriters would sit in different areas of the agency building. The copywriter would come up with a slogan; the slogan would be handed to the art director; and the art director would separately add graphics to the slogan.

Advertising legend Bill Bernbach changed that. He put the copywriter and art director in the same room, working on ideas together. The results spoke for themselves in legendary ads like

Volkswagen's "Think small" campaign. It took the rest of the advertising industry another seven years to pick up on this idea. Today, every agency is made out of those creative teams. They always come in two. Some teams spend their whole careers together and have been working together longer than being married to their spouses (I am looking at you, Tony and Guy).

When I was hired to bring innovation to a variety of agencies, it was nearly impossible to update or improve this. The silos were too strong. It was bittersweet to hear the story of Bill Bernbach and see how an industry can have the right idea but, half a century later, be intellectually blind to a variation of the same idea. I am not Bill Bernbach, and many smart people are working at advertising agencies who would like to make similar improvements and also cannot. That only shows you how strong and damaging silos can be.

## POLYMATH BY TOOL

There are many ways to learn more than one skill, of course. We live in a world of deconstructed tools. This has created people who can look at twenty different areas of expertise at the same time, talk to a few million people from a variety of backgrounds for answers, all while they manage their time and finances, order lunch for the team, and book next week's travel and hotels. Tools are automated skills or can be, depending on how they are used.

The internet exponentially increased our ability to engage with any niche or piece of information that exists. Today in many countries, people can engage and activate more detailed knowledge than ever before. If we consider that people always had great potential, we are closer to activating that potential. Our modern tools enable every area our curiosity can think of. Second- and third-generation tools can filter and repackage the amount of knowledge to manageable states. Notifications, time management tools, and other workflow apps and services make it possible for us to multitask and work at the efficiency level of a classic team.

This means people can try twenty hobbies a week, drop nineteen a week later, and move on to another set of people and interests after that. If companies allow it, these new tools enable them to keep pace with those new dynamics and behaviors. Some of this deconstruction of society and its interests had been observed back in the early 1970s. As Alvin Toffler described the appearance of subcultures in culture and how they became ever more specific and diverse: "This is the social mobility of the future; not simply a movement from one economic class to another, but from one tribal group to another. Restless movement from subculture to ephemeral sub-cult describes the arc of . . . life."

Such tools are accessible to anyone. Esko Kilpi notes that "skills and effort" are not a tactic for success anymore. Are you capturing this fact when you consider capabilities in the modern workplace?

Modern tools are robots in a different shape. They both automate tasks. They all enable us and the more you master, the more you will be a polymath yourself. In my opinion and from my own experience, tools and robots won't kill my job; they will enable me to turn my role into a super-job. At a time when we are starting to hire scrum-masters to enable agile processes, we should create tool-masters to equip polymath teams with a smart set of modern tools.

I remember a discussion in school in the '80s on how much we should be allowed to use calculators to do math for us. I wonder how many jobs were lost because of calculators.

Over recent years, deconstructed tools has elevated the single progressive worker's value. Comparing the market evaluation of companies like Facebook against companies like General Motors shows the difference. New tools turn workers into polymaths, but they can only do so with workers who have a modern mindset.

I have managed global crowdfunding campaigns as a nearly one-man army. The reason I could do so is tools like Hootsuite, Mailchimp,

IFTTT, Automate.io, Grammarly and many more. They let me wire-up my ecosystem of activities, automate my tasks, send messages at pre-prepared times, and get notifications as I requested. They let me put products of a Kickstarter campaign into thirty-six countries and 130 communities in thirty days. They let me run a successful book crowdfunding campaign an hour a day in my afternoons. The flexibility of these tools is their greatest value. A locked-in system like Microsoft Office cannot match it, and when you need greater flexibility, the locked-in system needs to be removed.

## LEARNING IS BUST

Last year in 2018, I came across an article that announced Google, Apple, and IBM are just some of the companies that do not require a college degree for their workers anymore. Their focus has shifted to people who have attended code camps or other opportunities outside of traditional educational institutions.

Stack Overflow is an extensive website for developers to ask and answer each other's questions. The site is an excellent, comprehensive reflection of the coding community. Its annual survey shows clearly that most coders learn new languages by themselves with online help, rather than learning around a traditional institution or workshop. If this indicates any trend, it is that learning never stops and traditional institutions provide less and less of the learning happening on this planet.

Back when I was in school in the '70s, I was told to find the one thing that I was good at and stick to it until I die. The educational system for my generation had good basics but lacked the insight to tell me that I would be learning all my life. When crafts and guilds were popular, people used to learn for a lifetime. Few remember this. In Germany, the traveling years of carpenters and Japanese traditions like calligraphy or sword-making are all built on the idea of continuous learning as part of everyday work.

Market trend analyst Scott Galloway, who has been observing the big corporates and their markets, has some simple advice: "Be remarkable. Develop not just one area of expertise, but two skills that don't always naturally go together. Be the CFO who also understands what music should be played at your events."[35]

It is hard for big classic companies to activate a workforce that was never expected to amend its mindset. In the last twenty-five years, I have worked in creative and advertising, banking, education, automotive, healthcare, entertainment, telecom, luxury, and various technology areas such as smart city and energy. I have been a designer, programmer, manager, and innovation specialist. Companies often say they need me yet are not comfortable with my eclectic views—with the new mindset. This also means that more than ever, my projects in companies have to include some form of applied learning. What has also been a trend is to more and more go from learning separately to learning by doing on real-world projects. It is tough, but I am amazed to see how many people can do it, despite their initial reservations.

As Toffler remarked, "Failure to diversify education within the system will simply lead to a growth of alternative educational opportunities outside the system."

You might say that nature will find its way to break an artificial silo. The information age has given us the opportunity to think broader, deconstructed, and beyond constraints. There is so much learning content on YouTube, Stack Overflow, professional platforms like Udemy, or niche sites like the RPF, where people can find very detailed advice on how to solve problems. (Don't ask me how I was able to build a reasonably accurate DL-44 blaster within a year in my kitchen.) Modern learning is already happening; it just isn't distributed evenly.

Learning different things is like learning multiple languages. They all provide a different view of a different part of our reality. Complex problems that affect multiple people involve multiple realities and need as many languages to solve. Children should be taught about the variety of language they will come across in their lifetime. Every new language is a bit easier. Stanford professor Carol Dweck makes the case of teaching a growth mindset, which articulates that intelligence is not innate, and all people are capable of learning and growth if we adopt a different mindset.[36]

For many years I have been interpreting between technologists and creative people. The languages don't easily align. In most of my recent projects, the language between business, design, and different siloed departments have impeded true collaboration and success. While the language of service design and enterprise architecture complement each other, I have found it can be hard to align in reality.

Understanding and aligning to a common goal requires a lot of energy. Often projects fail to anticipate this. Enable your business to tap into new ways of learning so that people are enabled to learn consistently. Even the *Harvard Business Review*[37] realizes the future of work lies in a cross-disciplinary approach.

Our educational system has been shaped by the industrial era. As Toffler notes:

> *The solution was an educational system that, in its very structure, simulated this new world [of factory workers] . . . The whole idea of assembling masses of students (raw material) to be processed by teachers (workers) in a centrally located school (factory) was a stroke of industrial genius. The whole administrative hierarchy of education, as it grew up, followed the model of industrial bureaucracy. The very organization of knowledge into permanent disciplines was grounded on industrial assumptions. Children marched from place to place and sat in assigned stations. Bells rang to announce the changes of time.*

## HIRE LIKE A POLYMATH

Entrepreneurial skills are not just a way to excite and sell an idea, but skills that connect horizontally. If silos become more commoditized through automation and processes evolving, companies need to hire horizontally. If we have commoditized a world via silos, then the new opportunities live between verticals. Horizontals will get us there.

Even longtime dot-com managers like Marissa Mayer of Google and Yahoo have hired based on vertical specializations. This echo of the Industrial Revolution is not aligned with the new ways of building a business anymore.

Startup investors have subconsciously shown a way to hire polymaths. Startup teams need to be flexible in their skills. Each member has to have at least three jobs combined within them. They need to learn fast and outside their first silo. Investors have to assess quickly if the team can do that, so they look for attitude rather than years of experience. In many articles and from my experience at startup pitches, investors consider team dynamics as a higher value than specialist skills. I believe they have the right idea—people, not tools. I have heard people in business complaining that all students bring is theoretical knowledge but no real experience. But if so, why should it be an issue that someone has to learn while they are working?

One of the significant challenges is to spot and identify what diversity of skills people have. Human resources departments are having a hard time hiring differently. The business paper "Asymmetric Information and Entrepreneurship"[38] concludes that asymmetric information about ability leads existing companies to employ only "lemons," relatively unproductive workers. Asymmetric here means that companies are unable to read "signals" in a CV that indicate highly productive or entrepreneurial types because characteristics such as resiliency, curiosity, agility, resourcefulness, pattern recognition, or tenacity don't often show up in a CV. The reason for this is that you could classify them as horizontal skills.

These overarching capabilities often work perpendicular to silo skills, like preferring one software tool over another or one process over another. These skills tend to ignore restrictions. This is why they are often found in entrepreneurs and not in the average siloed worker. Companies consistently fail to identify highly productive people because they hire vertically rather than horizontally.

Steve Blank, the originator of the Lean Startup Movement, observes: "Their recruitment and interviewing processes . . . are still focused on execution, not entrepreneurial skills."

Outcome and execution are different things. We need to start describing skills and projects with an outcome in mind, not with the solution set in stone. Industrial Revolution processes are set up like that: *Don't think and keep producing the same thing I always want from you.*

People have been trained to duplicate and manufacture the same thing in the same amount of time so that management can plan how the future will look. This does not work anymore; we need flexible people.

As business strategist Esko Kilpi says, we need to nurture people, especially in the absence of an educational system that has caught up with this new paradigm. We can't wait for twenty years or more. We need to deconstruct our workforce's workers, enable them, and nurture them.

# THE 1,000 FACES OF INNOVATION

**The new definition of billionaire is he [or she] who will positively affect the lives of a billion people.**

−Jason Silva

The scope and structure of teams are changing. Tame companies have been struggling to create self-organizing teams for some time now. The result is crippled innovation or failed attempts at it.

There is a struggle between system thinking's theory X and theory Y[39] for where governance sits, where support for the team sits, and who can get it. Theory X believes that people want to avoid work until they are pressured to do so. This is the purpose layers of management. It is mostly becoming obsolete and inefficient—or to put it more politely, its purpose has changed. Theory Y believes that people like to be self-organized and reach their true potential only then. We live in a world of theory Y, and beyond that, teams are becoming self-managed and self-organizing beyond initial team constraints. This is changing the way we perceive roles, skills, and governance and how we create value. It is changing teams' awareness of business drivers and models. These are wicked teams.

## THE FIRST TWELVE FACES OF INNOVATION

IDEO is famous for excellent product design. For decades, its solutions had an emotional layer that seemed to understand the user to a degree few companies could match. But it is not just a leader in human-centered design; its ways of working are as innovative as its designs. In 1984, Tom Kelley wrote a pivotal book[40] about typologies of team members and their dynamics. He described IDEO's a way of building teams where the designer is not always the designer, and the leader is not always the leader. The approach appreciated that people had multiple skills and could perform differently depending on their team or project context.

I have experienced this for many years. I have worked on many teams in very different roles: strategy, creative, and production. The first time I noticed I adapted to a team context was when I moved between teams that were either creative- or technology-heavy. Even though I am the same person, for the creative crowd I would be the technologist. For the technology crowd, I would be the creative or artist type. In each team, I provided the skills that were missing, balancing its expertise and making the output more holistic. Any problem should be observed holistically. If the balance is not there, impact and quality will suffer. Sometimes this will add to the risk of the project. Sometimes it will make the difference between fixing hygiene factors and creating a solution everyone will talk about.

Most companies lean toward design, engineering, or economics; few are genuinely balanced. In extreme cases, social media people will steer every solution toward Twitter campaigns and ironmongers will consider metal as the best material to solve a problem.

**If all you have is a hammer, everything looks like a nail.**

—Abraham Maslow

## Insanity is repeating the same mistakes and expecting different results.

### —Narcotics Anonymous (attributed to Albert Einstein)

Both the above quotes have come up in presentation slides a lot lately. They are the reason Microsoft is creating products with hundreds of features and Apple has a focus on design. They are why Facebook struggled to conquer mobile. Balancing company output to build the best product or service requires flexible teams who can adopt new skills and new knowledge iteratively.

One of my transformation projects managed to do just that. We were briefed to create new processes via new services via new teams with new capabilities. This meant we needed to teach service design methodologies and how to build business cases to teams mainly of engineers, who had never done such a thing. It was tough, and activities had to be guided, but we did not waste time on workshops. We learned on real projects with real targets. The business had change fatigue, so some teams were very skeptical. However, the energy was there, and when the first research data came in showing new insights and providing information to pivot and create valuable business cases, the mindset changed. The experiential and applied way we worked gave people the opportunity to grab the role they felt they could do. Some stayed within their comfort zone; some embraced new areas of expertise that no capability map could have predicted.

It was a beautiful proof of IDEO's principle at work. It also showed that the way businesses think they can train might not be the right way. It showed there are tons of hidden potential not accounted for in every company. Realizing the potential for multiple skills and flexible use of team members in projects is, in my opinion, one of the biggest opportunities companies are missing. The twelve faces of innovation explore various roles for individuals to take on in a project. Instead of describing team members by tools or skills,

Tom Kelley lists a range of archetypes responsible for outcomes of a project. *Outcome-based* is the keyword to look for here.

A good metaphor would be stem cells. Stem cells can create any type of cell functionality required given a specific context. If you believe in system Y, you will believe people can rise to the occasion, within reason. Tools further enable capabilities. Given the tools and processes we have today, having a workforce that acts like stem cells rather than siloed grains is the future of capability management and more possible than ever. Being iterative does not stop at how you atomize parts of your delivery; it goes all the way down to what people can do and learn.

IDEO has been able to do this in its sector. Given what I have seen in many innovation projects, startups, and transformation efforts, I think it safe to say there is a huge demand for workforces to provide this flexibility. The potential is there. All you need is to look at it from a wicked perspective. A tame company will expect everyone to stick to their skills, hire expensive consultants or acquire specialist companies, and do that again every two to five years. Tame companies dock on new things until they are too heavy to move. Wicked companies stay lean, learn, and adapt.

Rachel Higham, BT IT's managing director, stated that their biggest challenge is to quickly spin up outcome-based teams. BT is a large organization and a perfect example of a tanker that is hard to redirect. But Rachel understood it was not about tools anymore. It was possible to change course by focusing on mindset and the way it engaged with the world. A cultural change like this needed a leader with clarity, and it took Higham fifteen years to build up the right opportunity to put all this to a test.

When I interviewed her for the book, her assessment of the situation was not too surprising, but its clarity meant that the project had a direction with purpose:

- BT Technology needed a flexible, fundable pool of resources
- 13,000 specialists resources were locked into BAU
- Their context and frame of reference for solutions was very narrow
- BT, like other companies, had spent the last twenty years forcing its people to become highly specialized, now they were saying *We don't want that anymore, we want you to be able to do operations, do design and be commercial thinkers*
- The organization knew it needed to remove layers of management and turn some into enablers, not checkers of checkers

"This meant we needed to turn existing resources into polymaths and constant learners and we succeeded," Higham says. "The Da Vinci program is one BT's most successful cultural and people transformation programs."

The CIO of the Salvation Army removed its IT department to have IT capabilities spread across the rest of the business as a layer and not a silo. NHS digital did the same with service design. Centers of excellence or centralized capabilities can have the same effect as roles that are too inflexible and therefore become too self-important. If you manage every design task through a bottleneck that is the door to the design department, then you will be tame: a company has to scale and be agile.

As one CIO said, "I don't see any great need to have a specialist department when IT pretty much permeates each and every part of the business. IT services have increasingly become a commodity product and probably don't need too many technocrats anymore."

Tim Carmichael, ex-CDO of the British Army, stated very clearly that future challenges would only be solved by horizontal teams. Spotify is another example where teams have the flexibility to use different tools and a process they can tailor to their needs. One size doesn't fit all. None of the fourteen services during one of my transformation projects used precisely the same process. The outcome is what matters. Using team and tools in any way that works best creates a fantastic impact and performance.

Outside of mass production and manufacturing, I believe that flexibility trumps cloning or a cookie-cutter approach every time. Some have argued that a cookie-cutter approach—where templates and process rule every team—saves money, but if self-learning and adapting to new challenges is the day-to-day business for the team, they become more efficient with the same effort as any other team. This means in wicked companies, cookie-cutter is no improvement.

At other companies like IBM, the improvement lies in creating career paths for design-driven roles to give capabilities space to grow. When I was talking to Doug Powell, IBM's VP of design, he elaborated on driving new capabilities into better positions by creating equal career paths to different professions.

About half a century ago, social psychologist Warren Bennis considered a new type of company: "What, then will be the characteristics of the organizations of a super-industrial society? . . . there will be adaptive, rapidly changing temporary systems." – Warren Bennis

Bennis believed we would solve future problems with taskforces of strangers with a set of diverse professional skills, who can meet temporarily. I believe he described wicked teams.

In 1972, Dr Herbert Gerjuoy, a psychologist at the Human Resources Research Organization, noted that organizations need "situational groups," a term that is analogous with "outcome-based teams." Not only that, but what are the internet and its communication channels if not a collection of "situational groups?" Blogs, forums, and timeline-based conversations let people gather temporarily, discuss, join, and contribute. These gatherings often dissolve within hours. Their themes and memes are not unlike Kickstarter campaigns, which exist for thirty days to ensure a product's funding. Teams meet globally on video chats for day-long workshops. In short, the future has enabled "situational groups," and it is slowly trickling into companies' requirements to keep up with what some outliers have already mastered.

Now imagine automating that. What type of company would result? What would its platform look like? How do your HR activities support this sustainably? Wicked teams have deconstructed from capabilities into knowledge to be acquired and gathered around tasks needed to be done.

## SUPPORT

No team succeeds in isolation. Progressive and outcome-based teams work deconstructedly and iteratively. They will learn and bring in knowledge and capacity on demand. The support system they need requires the same characteristics.

Tools should be made available to produce the most effective way of working. Subject matter experts from across the business and outside should be available to gather insights and help with anything outside the team's expertise. Budgets need to be flexible. Strategic and supportive stakeholders needs to be accessible. Technology has for a long time realized than an open and free flow of knowledge and access creates exponential synergy. Business need to do the same to support its outcomes.

Most people who work for larger companies have observed a lack of support for decades. The market has finally progressed enough to put huge pressure on many companies to think more agilely and supporting their teams and efforts in different ways. Progressive or outcome-based teams have reduced that challenge by incorporatin a more complex and cross-disciplinary set of skills, but teams cannot perform in a vacuum, and neither can a startup or CEO. Finance, legal, company ecosystem, and a frictionless partnership network all can support the complexity of a project. I have often seen these support systems be the make-or-break of my projects. Wicked companies keep these aspects eclectic and agile so that projects can flourish in any way needed.

Startups might make headlines with millions of dollars being given to them, but the reality is that this happens in phases, tied to KPIs, OKRs, and other targets. Classic companies have budgets tied up in silos and by time instead of being outcome-based and available when projects need them.

Advertising has long been struggling with the appearance of technology platforms and the change in customer behavior around them. Messaging and stories have become more immediate and short-lived with higher impact. The fast pace of social media, in particular, put significant pressure on the tame mindset of agencies to change how they created and published the narratives of a brand. Campaign budgets, planning, and development can take months to be signed off. TV ads are high-end production efforts. Social media narrative, by contrast, is created on a phone, spikes within twenty-four hours and is forgotten the week after. Sign-off processes between client and agency could not compete with that. Some of that changed with the now famous Oreo Super Bowl tweet from 2013.

When the power in the football stadium went out, a creative team created and published a tweet within minutes that said, "You can still dunk in the dark." It caught over 6,000 likes and nearly 16,000 retweets. That much impact with that little investment was unprecedented. Some months later, the advertising industry had a name for it: newsroom marketing. The idea was to deconstruct budgets and sign-off time. By doing that, brands could react and piggyback on existing media waves like the Super Bowl, royal weddings, or other cultural events. If the content were contextual, if it related to the event, it would be shared and read by thousands.

Many tried to replicate this lean and effective way of reaching customers. I remember at Leo Burnett during the London Olympics, we managed to turn daily photos of the audience into billboard themes within an hour. This was groundbreaking for clients like McDonald's, opening up new ways to reach audiences and be relevant.

This success of newsroom marketing created some more interesting companies like New York-based Sparks & Honey. This data-driven service scans an incredible amount of internet traffic and data. Through its filters and machine-learning algorithm, it can detect trends and cultural memes, then report them back to clients as predictions and opportunity proposals to plant their narratives along culturally relevant waves. Today, Sparks & Honey has expanded its offer and applied its trend algorithm to other areas. The deconstructed nature of messaging platforms and other data tools has enabled these kinds of micro-reactions, impressively cheap to produce and test. If one fails, the repercussions are very minor, given the short attention span those platforms hold. This is what wicked companies are all about—having processes that enable changes and fast reactions to be sustainable.

A less deconstructed yet excellent example of a build-up effect of smaller investments is Coca-Cola's "Share a Coke" campaign that originated in Australia. If you remember people's names on Coca-Cola bottles or cans, you have seen this campaign. You can find its video on YouTube, and it will look like a big campaign planned from back to front. This couldn't be further from the truth. I bumped into Coca-Cola's CMO at a conference where he shared some insights into how the campaign became such a big deal. It only started with the idea to put 150 of the most popular Australian names on the bottles in a few shops. They had a small budget for it, produced a small batch of bottles, and hoped for the best. The impact of that first round was very high on social media; people tried to find the shops that had the bottles. So, the company spent more money on expanding the list of names. The campaign grew more, so Coke decided to have pop-up shops—temporary locations—where people could have their name printed onto a bottle. They kept increasing the campaign step-by-step, as long as people got excited and showed that they wanted more. They added billboards and let people put their names on them, and had a Christmas special. The campaign won a Cannes award for impact, and Coke used it in other countries like the UK, where I came across it at the agency I was working in at the time. It was one of the most effective ways to grow a campaign by iteratively adding to the budget and building on an ever-growing community of fans, rather than to create buzz starting from zero every time.

Just as with many other phenomena in our new technology-driven culture, the value in both examples is not in being connected, but in being able to create a deconstructed yet interdependent opportunity space. To be able to produce in such an iterative and agile way, budgets and sign-off processes need to have characteristics that align with these ways of working.

Platforms like Kickstarter succeeded in a different way. They cut out the middlemen of shops and distributors and created a proof-of-concept and PR tool that helps test ideas. The initial effort for bigger or established companies has in some cases become so expensive, none of these ideas would be considered. Creating a team, time, and funding around an idea has become very tricky. A more flexible support system can bring some of these opportunities back. The success of Kickstarter, Indiegogo, and others have evolved the market. Beyond donation-based crowdfunding, where people only pay for the product received, equity-based crowdfunding platforms like Crowdcube have introduced deconstructed ownership for an idea. These platforms have made it possible for companies like Pycom to launch their products directly to their customer community and get an exact idea of how many units they need to create to sell everything they produce. Venture capital firms and other investors have taken notice as well and carefully observed the company's performance on crowdfunding platforms as indicators for minor-risk investments. Following that, a successful crowdfunding campaign often guarantees a higher second-round investment. Creating a support system that can test an idea through lean or small-batch investment is very low-risk. A simple proof of concept or proof of interest via an essential communications effort has become a very lean way to test ideas. Simple tools like a one-minute video or poster are like how Google examines the initial adoption of an idea. Putting an idea out there in a simple way is often more valuable than expensively testing it within your product department. A support system should, rather than hinder you, allow you to put something out there to test.

Support systems for ideas can come in all shapes. At London's Science Museum, we created the UK's first crowd-led content testing platform. In 2009, the antenna gallery opened to showcase science news on the ground floor. The initial idea was a gallery within a gallery—a space that would highlight a science story alongside exhibits, an elaboration of a single story to tell a bit more than a simple news article can tell. Usually, the curators would pick what story to highlight and expand.

Antenna Gallery did something different. Through a couple of exhibition hubs and smaller installations, we introduced daily news stories. Those could be liked, voted on, or commented on, and we used that visitor information to learn what stories people were most interested in. We picked the article that got the most attention and turned it into a mini-exhibition within Antenna Gallery, which itself became a small media platform to help curate news stories and facilitate visitor interest. Sometimes it pays to develop your form of publishing to gather feedback and test interest.

The last two examples both happened during my work for Leo Burnett, a global advertising agency. Working for P&G and Kenco, an instant coffee maker, we were able to tap into their business networks. In both cases, we connected to their innovation departments. In both, we faced budget and timing constraints. A good client relationship and some confidence got my team to talk to parts of the client's company an advertising company wouldn't usually talk to. This let us open up silos that the client itself wasn't able to break through.

We visited P&G's research facility in Egham, a candy shop for great ideas and technology to use in our campaigns. The partnerships and capabilities they provided were extraordinary. We walked away with technology solutions for our existing project and dozens of ideas for our upcoming campaigns already funded by their research facility. For one idea, P&G gave us access to its 3D specialist, who had done special skin effects for the movie *Avatar.*

Kenco's mother company, Kraft, picked up the budget for our technology build via its innovation hub in the U.S. It was a European first for an interactive vending machine called Kenneth. Feel free to google Kenneth, the talking vending machine: it got shortlisted for the most emotionally impactful campaign that year.

In 2003, Nicholas G. Carr wrote a pivotal article called, "IT Doesn't Matter."[41] In one of his statements that commented on the difference of IT from other company assets, he wrote, "Infrastructural technologies, in contrast, offer far more value when shared than when used in isolation."

Your teams are only as good as their support system. If you create a new business process, make sure support is part of your roadmap. A drip-feed finance system, specialists, ways to publish and test, access to potential customers, long- and short-term strategy and research—there are many roads to success. Create the right soil in which efforts can grow.

# TOWER OF BABEL

New and old professions have created a complex new set of languages. Every language's ambition is to describe the world around it within the mindset that defined the practice. However, languages can be silos, creating friction and inefficiencies. Because wicked companies are aiming for zero friction, languages need to be open and accessible. Finding a universal language for problem solving from top to bottom is a task every company should perform.

Every practice goes through knowledge evolutions. Anyone who worked in a job for more than a few years has seen different frameworks and ideas on management, production approaches, communication principles and rules, ways of working, and ways of expanding what contributes to someone's area of expertise and role within projects. As a developer, I have seen computer languages and their frameworks arrive and disappear. As a manager, I went from PRINCE2 to Agile. New things come with new differentiating languages. I love learning new things, but in terms of project efficiency, these different languages make collaboration and agreement on value and process often time-consuming and inefficient.

The need for cross-disciplinary teams will likely increase. The clash of languages that need to align is inevitable. If we want to solve complex problems better, we need to simplify the way we share knowledge and accept each other's mental and value models in which we describe the context within which we work.

My current focus is on transformation for businesses. My language of choice is design thinking. It is a newly renamed profession and I am using a variation of it. It has its origin in human-centered design and it is rapidly evolving. It preaches inclusiveness but is not without flaws in that approach. I was recently asked to share my observations on how it could evolve. The answer can be complex.

Service design is not the only language for problem solving. The array of tools, models, and processes out there is often confusing. It also wastes time and money translating between duplicate efforts and agreement on definitions. This is an opportunity for service design to be the centerpiece for an agile universal language.

Back in 1999, I thought that within five years every designer would also be a coder. Eighteen years later, this has not happened. Instead, new tools, processes, and disciplines have appeared, shifted, and merged. Helping companies be their best selves has become not only more complex, but also a more crowded market. Clients are likely to suffer among the multitude of languages, processes, and tools they are expected to implement. Service designers have always been promoters of inclusion and simplicity. They should practice what they preach and embrace our friends from enterprise architecture, systems thinking, business analytics, and others to develop a more inclusive and intuitive way to talk about the process of problem solving, not just for customer-facing problems, but across all of business.

## COMPLEXITY CYCLES

Service design is not the only discipline that went through a complexity cycle when it matured. Macromedia Flash, later Adobe Flash, started as a software solution to do vector animations on the internet around 1999. It introduced a coding language called ActionScript to make vector-based websites interactive and experiential. Flash-based websites boomed, because they provided unique and engaging user experiences on the Web, which was previously a very static affair.

ActionScript evolved. It started with a few simple commands, written in near English, and a very formalized, restricted way of putting code pieces together. You wouldn't even write code words—you just clicked on buttons to add simplified modules. Version 2.0 had free text coding, just like any other web-based script language. Version 3.0 had libraries, classes, frameworks, and had become so complex that one could code game engines with it. People started to create third-party ActionScript editing tools to manage its complexity better. The community had its conferences, events, and accreditations.

I was at one of those conferences around 2004 when a speaker made a valid point about its complexity. Back in version 2.0, some basic functionality took three lines of code, easily understood and accessible to artists and creative people who had never coded before and had brought a fantastic amount of exploration and new thinking to the community. Version 3.0 needed a list of classes and libraries to be added to the code and initiation code around that to do what was previously done in three lines of code. The community had evolved from an open, inclusive one to an exclusive specialist one. It had replaced evolution with complexity.

A year or two later, Flash got replaced by HTML5 and its capabilities, and ActionScript died a slow quiet death. The same could currently happen to service design, but it could avoid this by simplifying and being more accessible. I would expect it to grow like ActionScript because at its heart it is inclusive, agile, iterative, and able to solve problems inside organizations and outside.

## SIMPLICITY ADOPTS QUICKER

Late last year I took part in Jake Knapp's Google Sprint course at the Barbican in London. I had just finished creating a Service

Design Center of Excellence for BT and had taught and set up an environment that offers service design to everyone. I had done dozens of workshops and was curious how he would be able to squeeze a week's workshops into a single day. Most participants were not designers but could identify a problem and create a solution to be tested using a straightforward decision-making process. There is a lot to be said about the way Google Sprints deals with customer research and the risk of getting it wrong. The mantra of "fail fast" is compelling, both for people and for the companies adopting an accessible methodology without fancy tool names and formalized print-outs and post-it mechanics; no unreadable blueprints.

I challenged him during a break about his thoughts on service design. He appreciates the discipline, but finds choosing from the large number of tools complicated and confusing, for both himself and the people he works with. Google Sprints show how service design could grow if it considers different levels of simplicity in its execution. The question here is what balance to strike between simplicity for ease of adoption and impact through a wide array of detailed tools. All of this will determine the complexity or simplicity of this new universal language.

## BLIND MEN AND AN ELEPHANT

Over the last few years, many disciplines have revealed themselves as very close to service design's ambition to improve business and its processes. Systems design, enterprise architecture, business analysis, and many others are all problem solvers working on the same problem. Having worked with them reminded me of the old Indian parable about the blind men and the elephant.

For those who don't remember, the story involves a group of blind men, who have never encountered an elephant. Each blind man touches one and only one part of the elephant's body. One touches the side, another the tail, another the tusk. They then describe the elephant based on their limited experience, but their descriptions disagree and they grow angry with each other. We tend to claim absolute truth based on our limited, subjective experience, but others' experiences may be equally true.

I believe businesses are changing and becoming more aware of their context and the processes available to them to thrive in the market. Our problem solving is becoming more holistic and collaborative. Currently, we are still going through the teething pains of new processes and teams because we are too tool- or role-focused.

A service designer from NHS Digital told a familiar story during the Dublin conference last year. What a service designer or a business analyst does in terms of internal processes can look like duplication of effort. The roles are actually complementary and using both creates a more complete picture of the problem to be solved. This benefit is often obstructed by role labels. The difference in language between service design and business analytics did not make the purpose of the service designer clear. It wasted time and money and created confusion across the team.

I have seen this in many projects myself. Tame silos are creating friction even in smaller projects. The big question is, therefore, who will help the blind men to work together, to combine their experiences and expertise to understand what the elephant is? Service design or a similar discipline should lead on this.

## MULTILINGUALITY

Science and universities are starting to realize the potential of combining multiple skills on a team basis or are actively encouraging students to have a second or third complimentary skill or interest area. The organizations are actively moving from the vertically siloed genius to the horizontally open polymath as a potential to solve our future. Science has already provided evidence that being in the top 25 percent of expertise in two or more areas has equal value than a lifetime of trying to be the very best in one silo. Athletes know that staying at the top and improving a few milliseconds in performance requires exponentially more energy with less and less benefit. There is a threshold here, where the level of improvement will not justify the energy and effort required.

Here and there, out of necessity, people are combining tools and processes, meanings, and mindsets to be able to work together. I can see glimpses of this, but they are often temporary and forgotten after a project has finished. If we start documenting these experiences, we could not just save time and money, we could learn, improve, and share so others won't have to learn the same things the hard way. If we understand we are all just part of the same problem-solving community, we might be able to do better things faster.

The self-driving car is a wicked problem. One of the ways Google is progressing fast is that all the cars share their data and learning among each other. This means every car anywhere will know what any other car knows and learns. We need to do the same.

I do not want to be biased about service design, but I am. In terms of opportunity I do not think it is any better or worse than other disciplines because I believe the future of solving problems will be a mix of things. But it represents an opportunity for mindset shift and transformation because it is part of the investment for tame companies to enter the wicked economy of services, experiences, and beyond. A quantitative-only approach will not give you enough insight into how your company can be a player in the experience economy. Design thinking and human-centered research create both qualitative and quantitative insights. If you are investing in taking them on board, consider introducing new ways of working and a new way of supporting your efforts. If you put research and insights in a silo, they will not be able to contribute to new value because they will not be ever-present across the process. They will be invisible by the time the solution reaches production and the live product will not be built with that insight in mind. I have seen this happen all too often. So if you are planning to bring service design or agile or systems thinking into your business, expand your strategy and investment to crack down on silos and bring other practices into the mix. Wicked companies are inclusive.

Sir Charlie Bean, ex-chief economist at the Bank of England, said that talking about manufacturing and services as distinct concepts is "very often not a helpful way to think about economic activity." In my view, he points out that creating a product in any shape or form is perceived as a value, whereas services are still struggling to be recognized as the value they create beyond customer satisfaction.

Desirability, viability, and feasibility (DVF) are the three mantras that service design embraces. Design is often known for its soft, empathic side. But being customer-centric does not mean ignoring business benefit. DVF proves that. Desirability is the customer side or internal staff benefit, viability is the business benefit case, and feasibility is the capability assessment. This means two-thirds of this design effort assessment, if it is valuable and can be done for and by the business. It is a very balanced approach. The more we aim to create a shared and simplified open language, the more likely we will be able to produce value that addresses all three aspects. As a business, you should have every team in any new project start by aligning their language. It might sound wasteful, but there is an easy exercise to show how problematic language can be:

Have the team sit together, and give everyone a piece of paper and a pen. Ask them to draw a vase. Have everyone hold up what they drew and observe the different picture everyone has. A vase is a simple thing. Now imagine how differently they will describe the project ahead of them.

Language matters. It brings clarity and reduces misalignment. It can create a shared purpose, which contributes to better solutions.

# VALUE CHANGE: TAME TO WICKED

**M**ost companies still believe that better technology will make them more competitive. Most transformation projects are only focused on IT and tooling. This is technology transformation, not mindset or cultural transformation. Technology has become a commodity, so pervasive it gives little extra margin or advantage to run on a different ecosystem. The differentiator is who is using the tools and what their mindset is. The other aspect is the context within which technology is used. What works in Japan might not work in Germany. How well you know the world you are creating it is another differentiator. No one invests in a value that can't be measured. New companies should measure and be measured and evaluated by the way they excel in all three areas, not just one.

In 1999, B. Joseph Pine II and James H. Gilmore proclaimed the experience economy, that experience would become a commodity. Alvin Toffler had indicated toward a similar trend when he wrote about the service economy back in the 1970s. Value added for a customer or user comes from the value existing inside a company or organization. The value and authenticity of a company are linked to the value it can create for customers or users.

Apple is very design driven. Microsoft is more driven by an engineering view on features and shows that in their product offering. I once had a near-philosophical debate with a Microsoft employee on why the early iPhone was good or bad. My arguments were based on designing for human behavior; his was on arguing that it did not have certain features that other devices had. The difference between what and how essentially showed the difference both companies have in why they do things.

Advertising agencies have alluded to an added value needed for tame companies for years. Their solution was for companies to expand their brand by superficially aligning with a cause, something like fighting poverty or cancer. The problem is that most people can spot a lack of authenticity from a mile away. If something does not align with the essence of your organization, it will reject it like the wrong type of organ replacement.

In 2004, Nicholas G. Carr commented on the commodification of technology in his pivotal book *Does IT Matter?* He argued there is nothing at all special about information technology, that it would go the way of the railroads, the telegraph, and electricity, which all became, in economic terms, just common factors of production, or "commodity inputs." "From a strategic standpoint, they became invisible; they no longer mattered," he wrote. It is now almost two decades later, and we are still putting a strong focus on features and technology as a differentiator. We need to expand and shift that mindset when we want to evaluate organizations and their output.

## SLEEPER AGENTS

A Gallup poll from 2013 showed that 63 percent of workers are not psychologically involved in their work. I would argue the more deskilled or tame a company structure is, the more it disengages workers. In any of the cross-disciplinary teams that I ever worked in, people learn more, are more curious, have more valuable conversations, and are more eager to keep things efficient and agile. There is a more significant perception of value and purpose across teams. Because the structure is horizontal, what matters at the top also matters to the team at every level. This brings clarity and a feeling of a shared effort. As a company, you should be able to investigate inside of roles and capabilities. In one of my transformation projects, we had to scan through multiple departments and thousands of potential candidates to find our initial teams for our pilots. We used qualitative and quantitative methods to do so. The quantitative aspect was using existing role descriptions and skill sets to get an idea of the person's potential. On the qualitative side, we handed out small surveys to see which people would tend to put more time in, work on separate ideas outside of office hours, and show interest in moving into different responsibility areas. The quantitative side could not tell us what type of designer we could get or how they would perform in a team setting. The qualitative side pointed us toward some of the most high performing and open mindsets within the company. People who measured high on the qualitative side were quick to learn and adapt and often showed team leader or polymath-like capabilities. Wicked companies are good at finding and attracting flexible and high-value people like this. Tame companies do not have the means to measure this value. I did a survey a few months ago to ask people how much of their skill sets and expertise they can bring into their current jobs. Most of the replies stated around 50 percent or less.

I have worked with many engineers and been one myself. There is a significant difference between prominent corporation engineers and startup engineers. They might have the same coding skills, but they will not have the same mindsets. Engineers with a tame mindset did not last long in startups; engineers with a wicked mindset will not stay at tame organizations. Because many big organizations have been tame for a long time but want to shift, they are beginning to try to find wicked engineers. A recent conversation with someone at Publicis Sapient made it quite clear that there is a high demand for wicked engineers coming. This will also be true for other practices as companies are slowly shifting.

Business consultant Esko Kilpi states:

> *The principles of extraction and simplification still apply to the social systems of work: most of our firms can be described as monocultures. We also do our best to productize humans to fit the job markets. One-dimensional social designs have the same built-in risks as original simplified designs. Extractive social systems can cause the same kind of damage to human ecology as mining, and other extractive systems have caused to the natural ecology. People truly are seen as "resources" and as such become dependent on artificial motivation systems, the human equivalents of fertilizers. We call them incentives.*

The added value of people being able to bring more of themselves into their job is what will give you the next edge. Many business leaders have said it is the people that make the company. If as a leadership team you can measure that value and bring it into your projects, it is not just customers or users who will benefit.

## AVENGERS ASSEMBLE!

Another flexibility or agility to measure is how quickly companies can align to required outcomes. Where there is inherent flexibility to be measured per person, on the team level you need to measure how fast you can assemble an outcome-based team. The definition of a wicked problem is that its context keeps changing. Agile and iterative processes and their tools can anticipate that to some degree, but people need to adapt to a change in context and be able to reassess existing and new data from a different viewpoint. The tools will be the same in a changing context. It is the world aspect and the mindset of the team that makes all the difference.

This is where agility can only allow a change in direction; it is research and the team and data from the world that will define why the change is necessary. In my last project, we were able to pivot some of the teams and strongly increase impact after launch. The ability to measure and show the value of the insight, reason to shift, and additional value afterward can show the importance of this flexibility. If you start measuring this new agility, you can invest better in becoming a wicked company.

If you can remove managerial layers and make teams more self-enabled, then you are adding organizational agility. If you consider that those teams can continuously learn and improve through testing and curiosity, then growth efforts are shifted and atomized into them. If you move strategy, finance, legal and other business specialization into slim support layers then there is one final question: What initial list is required from senior management?

Tim Carmichael, CDO of the British Army, reminded me of a military principle I had first read in L. David Marquet's pivotal book *Turn the Ship Around!*,[42] a record of a military nuclear submarine adopting system Y principles in management. The book explains the military concept of operational intent, which leaves the solution up to the executing team. It is not unlike a problem statement of service design. As usual, the similarities and differences between professions and their languages are fascinating. It is this intent that should populate a marketplace of wicked problems. Generate this intent, and open up this marketplace.

## SUPPORTED VALUE

Facebook has an employee value of $24 million, Google of $8 million, and Twitter about $5 million. Classic companies like VISA or Mastercard are still doing well with around $11 million per employee, and we know that these are not the most enabled companies. So the question remains: What makes a company efficient and how do we measure this new era of deconstructed flexibility?

In the support system of teams, the value of a person can become very complex, and it is worth tracking. A few years ago, I worked at an agency that employed a creative technologist. He was likely the most versatile coder they had on staff. He kept being pulled into many different projects because his skill set kept expanding. I remember throwing a hardware project at him, a rapid prototyping project. He just picked it up and delivered it, even though he had never done anything like it before. From one week to another, we were done. He was a bit more senior than others, so he had a higher salary, but he was probably worth double that. He didn't belong to a particular account team, so the budget for his job was not linked to any growing stable budget. I would have picked him first for any new outcome-based team. His tame company did not see his value, because it didn't measure value like that. He was the support system that enabled a lot of other teams. He kept other teams lean. He could use his knowledge and tools he learned from other teams in new teams. That was perhaps one of the reasons he was so versatile and efficient.

Support systems can be complicated when first instantiated. Every supported project and team needs to acknowledge and report its value back. In my current project, we are about to merge and align service journey modules. Three teams are working on similar experiences and using different parts of the ecosystem. Making extra time to align this will not be measured at this stage, but we will have to measure the reduction of duplication and additional simplicity that will reduce error, time, and investment. My current organization has been heavily siloed, but now it has three wicked teams.

A typical team member runs on multiple activity lanes and sits in a variety of different subject and practice groups, often created to support each other in activities and knowledge sharing. This means each can be part of a production and help another team or practice group. This is the start of role deconstruction and leaner layers of support. A tame company would push most of the teams to run in the same way. Our wicked company members aim at the same quality and run on the same purpose, but we interpret the process and support each other on a contextual basis. In an economy where experiences need to be personalized to a customer, creating exact copies of the last product as outputs is failing.

Esko Kilpi, thinker on progressive company structures and values, agrees. Evaluating companies on their modular potential rather than their efficiency, or on a mixture of both, would create a very different market.

Tim O'Reilly is not far from that thought. The world has bespoke design agencies, innovation agencies, sales agencies, PR, and marketing agencies tailored to startups. Who needs departments and a leadership team?

Democratic politician Howard Dean famously enabled his grass roots by decentralizing and deconstructing agendas for the local constituencies. It was a model later picked up by Barack Obama and others. Modern companies will be closer to the complexity of nature. Human beings are complex and have a multitude of purposes. Tame companies are artificial, simplistic constructs. Wicked companies are more diverse and eclectic and therefore more organic and sustainable.

# FIGHTING A SILVERBACK GORILLA

Change is hard. How long did your gym membership last? How long did it take you to drop that smoking habit? When was the last time you checked your email? It takes a lot of energy and many contextual factors for something to permanently change in one's life. Moving from tame to wicked is an enormous step, and it is healthy to know why that is and to let everyone else around you know as well.

I have not meant to give you the impression that a mindset that has evolved over fifty years is easy to adopt. I bumped into it twenty years ago, by accident. I didn't anticipate it and, trust me, I had headaches for months when I started master's degree studies in London and things just kept flooding in. At times, it is healthy to realize how big this step is. It likely will be a journey for you as it has been and still is for me. There are moments when I don't want to hear about yet another framework, tool, or interpretation of a term that I thought I had figured out, its meaning sealed.

It is not a matter of being smart. It is a viewpoint that anyone can consider. This is why many intelligent people have failed to see the modern world for its opportunities, but it is important to remind oneself that there are many defense mechanisms baked into our very existence that prevent new mindsets.

I have seen many of my like-minded colleagues quit jobs and leave their industries forever because they were hired for their expertise and then not listened to. I have seen companies struggle to take on required steps and failing not because of the technology or money, but because people could not adopt their views. Humans are not set up to change their views quickly. We are built to stay the course. Embracing a new view never comes easily to anyone. Knowing this can give us consolation, understanding, and energy when times are uncomfortable and feel strange.

## BREAKING THE MOST PRECIOUS THING

To some extent, we all love what we do. We might complain, but each of us still loves our job or the people or the sense of purpose it gives us or the achievements it occasionally gives us back, and sometimes it is the constant challenge that keeps our lives interesting. Now imagine someone took that away. This is what changing your mindset can feel like.

Think about New Year's resolutions. Gym memberships spike every January by 12 percent, but they drop shortly after. Do you have a dusty guitar in the corner that you aimed to learn how to play? How long did you stick to your last diet? We are creatures of habit. Marketing calls it *anchoring* when our first experience of something acts as an anchor for any following exposure of the same kind. What price do you consider for an expensive bottle of wine? Depending on your first bottle of expensive wine, it can be $10, $100 or $1,000. You will position any price for a bottle of wine afterward without thinking or reconsidering. The human species is averse to new thinking. You are not off the hook for behaving ignorantly; you should try to spend the energy a few times a year to review some of your "obvious" statements and habits. It is a good brain exercise.

In his 2012 book *Thinking Fast and Slow,*[43] Daniel Kahneman identifies two modes in our brain. The A brain relies on an existing library of thoughts and interpretations. It is our go-to guy when making sense of the world, the part we rely on 99.9 percent of the time, a low-power and "cheap" solution to our day-to-day needs and troubles. The A brain does not add any new findings to its library; it merely depends on existing knowledge. It is the part responsible for most of our survival. Faced with a sabretooth tiger, the human being who would carefully consider whether the animal is a threat was eaten a few million years ago. The A brain acts quickly and automatically. It never tries new stuff. It helped us survive, so it has earned its right to exist.

The B brain, in contrast, is an energy hog. It is our version of an iPhone battery, always needing more energy, so we rarely use it. If we do, its energy needs are so vast that we need to shut down other processes. Kahneman gives a striking example I have used on friends; you should try it too. Go for a walk with someone. Talk to them. You will be able to both walk and talk; talking still only uses the A brain. Now ask them a harder math question, like 12 times 36. Watch them stop walking. The B brain needs so much energy and focus it can't keep walking while doing math at the same time. The B brain is the thinking you need to do to add new ideas to your mind. We rarely use it. This is why we rarely invent new things or are open to new ideas. It is just too energy intensive.

After the Iraq War began, scientists did interviews with U.S. citizens who supported it and showed them proof that their president had lied to them about it. Most people had excuses and went to extreme lengths to justify why their initial assessment was correct and that the president couldn't possibly lie.

The same happened in a study where U.S. citizens were asked their opinion on same-sex marriage. When the facts they were shown were in line with their own opinion, they agreed with the facts and praised them as facts. When confronted with opposing facts, people declared those facts irrelevant to this particular subject.

There has been a long discussion especially in recent U.S. political punditry about "fake news" and the discrediting of facts on either side of more and more polarized debate. Both sides claim opponents ignore the facts or are lying. Maybe we need to acknowledge that there is not an absence of fact, but an absence of flexibility or openness to different opinions. This shows how hard it is to shift a mindset.

Thanks to anchoring, the first number you hear is the most relevant. For price negotiations, if you start at $1,000, the rest of the conversation will be anchored around this initial number and its perception by each party involved. As far as I understand, the black swan theory is based on the same kind of anchoring. A black swan is something that is considered very rare to the extent that it is unthinkable. Most people know swans to be white. Imagine if the first swan you saw was black.

All this is summarized in a phenomenon called cognitive bias, which is any CIO or startup CEO's worst nightmare. Statistically, everyone will disagree with you no matter what. Unless both parties are willing to step into B brain mode, you will not make progress. This is where LEGO comes in. I am using LEGO as a synonym for some of the activities and tools that design thinking or innovation workshops are using. They might look flimsy from the outside, but are very powerful when you are in the middle of it. There is a reason why consultancies drag you outside your office building: different physical context and dynamic primes you to use your B brain.

Some activities need simple icebreakers for everyone to feel comfortable and to establish that anything silly is okay for today. LEGO is an icebreaker and productive activity in one. We all know LEGO and what to do with it, so we are not uncomfortable around it. We know that the essence of playing with this toy is imagination and building something imperfect but fun. The abstraction level of the toy lets people reexplore familiar scenarios and look at things in a new way. These sessions are not teaching you something new. They are showing you something old that you knew as a child, which is to look at the world as a new thing. It is a brain hack to get you back into your childhood, when you used your B brain more often.

There is probably a reason why a kid's heart rate is higher and they need more extended sleeping hours. They are continually running on B brain to analyze and make sense of their context. Most things need to be considered with high energy because they are new.

Kahnemann explains how badly cognitive bias can disable people's perception of reality. In one experiment, they had a couple of joggers following another jogger showing symbols on his or her back via a simple screen he was wearing. They had to remember the signs the front man showed. While they were jogging in public, the researchers had a man dressed up as a gorilla run through the joggers and along with them. After the run, the joggers were asked if they saw the gorilla. They did not. The brain utterly ignored it. This is why new mindsets and insights can hide in plain sight.

One can imagine the impact of this on business. Innovation and transformation consultancies are working hard to break this pattern. I wonder if they would manage their expectations right if they knew it is biologically hard to change. So imagine how perceptive you would be to a problem that behaves differently after you started working on it. Would you notice? Would you have processes in place that prepare for that? Would you have a team that is aware of that when it starts measuring success?

Most frameworks, languages, and methodologies we have in place are trying the same thing. They all simplify reality to make the right decisions. If you have one or multiple ones in place, why improve on it? You know reality, you have seen the numbers, and you have more important things to do, like fixing what's wrong. I think it was Einstein who said that 50 percent of the solution is knowing what the problem is in the first place. He did not say that if he had one hour to save the world, he would spend 59 minutes to understand what the problem is and one minute on the solution, but whoever said those things described wicked problems.

To overcome this bias, all you can do is overcommunicate. You might think of a change of mindset as a movement. A clear purpose and a good set of principles people can agree to is a crucial starting point. They will create a narrative that excites early adopters and helps everyone else understand why it would matter and help to participate. Keep your message simple. Talk to your supporters first. Companies that explore new things need their early adopters. They are the people likeliest to already agree with you—the low hanging fruit.

These things cannot be overcome by money. The right and most valuable people will join despite time and money restrictions. This is how dominant a mindset can be once you activate it. This is why recognizing the size of the challenge is so important. You will have failures along the way. Recognizing that things will be tough makes it easier to get back up and try harder.

Many years ago, doing my bachelor's degree, I started to move from drawing to painting. I had only done line drawing and was very new to what color could do to my creative mindset and expression of it. I was not sure if it was for me. In my painting course, I was to create a painting on a canvas, with brushes and paint. An empty canvas is not unlike an open brief. "Create something new." Where to start? Anything?

"Choose three objects; that's the only rule for this exercise," said my professor, a very successful local painter, back in 1998 in Hamburg. Out of a billion ideas, which three objects would make sense to me? I picked three in my head. As every writer or artist knows, an empty canvas or piece of paper can be an intimidating thing. The first cut is the deepest; the first step is the hardest. I started painting a chair (how cliché), a glass bottle (very empty), and a lightbulb (Aha!). How to lay them out on the canvas? I sketched it up somewhat and checked the proportions to something I hoped would make it look interesting. At the end of a two to three-hour session, I had used some color and had started to fill the canvas somewhat. It took me over the coming week to get to a point where I had added more detail and developed some style. Not too realistic, a bit abstract, but not Picasso-level abstract. Over the coming weeks, I repainted the objects and added different levels of detail and contrast to make it look like a proper painting, whatever that meant. When you paint, you sometimes want to direct the viewer's eye to specific points of your creation. I tried that. My professor would stop by briefly to pick on the weaknesses of my creation: my lack of experience was seemingly evident.

After a few more weeks and hours of working, I considered it in an excellent state. I had taken photos each day to revisit and document my progress and process. I was proud; I had created something that looked like a painting. My first real painting; hours of work, tons of thinking and doing.

"That's very good," my professor said, and I was so proud.

"Now destroy it!" was his next sentence.

My immediate reaction was confusion. Why would I possibly do this? What purpose would this have?

As he explained, in a creative process it is essential to know when to stop. In theory, one can paint on a painting forever. Keep adding, keep changing, keep exploring, and keep learning while creating. Some artists do this. Most stop at some point when they are happy enough with the result, but how do you know when to stop? Is it just a gut feeling or can it be learned?

I was about to learn. It was a hard lesson to learn. Imagine taking a brush to a finished masterpiece. My painting was no masterpiece, but it was my baby I had worked on for weeks. It had tremendous value for me. I was about to destroy something that I could not get back.

I did, and I learned. There is a liberating feeling after you have stepped over a certain point after you have jumped headfirst into uncertainty. A few things will never be the same. When you go freelance, when you are an entrepreneur for the first time, things start to look very different. Anyone who is a parent knows this. It is a big door that opens up. After more than twenty years on this journey,

I am aware that I have been privileged and lucky. But I am not unique; I think everyone can experience this; all it takes is the right context and feedback loop.

As a designer, I have seen my fear of destruction become manageable. The more I am dealing with it, the more I can deconstruct and verbalize the misconception from fear to excitement. Change is good, but I am aware of the reluctance and preconditioning others are part of.

The effort to change a mindset in people is the size of a gorilla or the elephant in the room. The more you acknowledge that the challenge is present and tough, the more you can make it appear smaller, laugh about when it doesn't go according to plan, or help each other when support is needed. During a one-year transformation project, I shifted all my energy to helping my teams. At some point, I did not produce anything for reports or to document the process. All my focus was on helping them through a tough time when more attention was needed. My communication with and support of the growing new community was more valuable than anything else I could have done. It was not because I thought they needed support, but because they asked me. We had established a dynamic where people could talk about their doubts and challenges. All I did was take action as fast as I could, and within a few weeks, we were at the top of our game. I will always be grateful to those teams and the fact that no one quit when things were on fire. This is overcommunicating in a good way. This is support.

# GOVERNMENT IS NEXT

Technology has slowly changed industry by industry. The speed of this trickle-down effect has been defined by the level of harm that can be done to people. There is an apparent last contender.

First, entertainment, music, and video were affected. Nobody dies if those get meddled with. Then came advertising and marketing, which still haven't realized what's going on, but that is another story. Then hospitality and social activities. People do stuff, but they generally can make that decision, and if the act doesn't show up or the scenario gets weird, one leaves or picks another hotel, and there you go. From that, we moved to automotive. Now we started talking about robot cars and digital car features. The second you could hack a car, you didn't want someone to go 120 kilometers an hour and fiddle with it. Lives started to matter, and the industry picked up slower.

At this stage, we also started evolving healthcare and finance. There is serious money in finance. Financial bots and cryptocurrencies are putting people's life savings in jeopardy, and the global economy might turn funny. Industries that by nature deal with more severe consequences of change and failure have always been slower in picking up on change. We have now reached financial, healthcare and insurance, serious business sitting in serious silos surrounded by legislation and entry-point investment thresholds. There is one piece missing, of course.

Government has exploited some of the new social tools, but not changed or improved itself. If we look at how easy it is to sign a petition—and I just signed as one of six million people that wanted to reassess Brexit—you could think about why voting and citizen engagement is not more citizen-friendly. Every other industry has progressed by getting rid of middlemen, either by automating or putting the consumer in new governance positions. This shift is overdue for the government.

Twenty years ago, it would have taken a big company and a lot of money to do the things everyone is now doing. The result of this is not just lower margins, as Jeremy Rifkin announces, but smaller batches. It has never been easier for a teenager in his or her parents' garage to start a supply chain to Shenzhen, China and supply the world with her invention.

Now apply this to government. In a world where complicated decisions should have bespoke, individual engagement, a new citizen contract and process should start to form. The main challenge is that government has a monopoly on government, on your identity and your vote. Currently, we have a system we only control once every few years, and even then we don't know what the control entities will do as there is a weird disconnect between what we voted for and what they have actually to do. Oddly enough for everything else, including the Oscars, there are tools in place that let us interact and vote in real time on every little piece of modern culture.

Can we remove the middlemen? That would mean the politicians. The governance and power structure will shift, but I believe it is the right time to look at alternatives to representational democracy and an individually bespoke democracy. Are politicians the smartest people to make the most intelligent decisions? They are undoubtedly great salespeople. If YouTube gives us a film studio and a celebrity channel platform; if Uber is your chauffeur, who will provide to turn a citizen vote into a society outcome? What if anyone could be a politician tomorrow? What is a politician today for us? What should it be?

I added this thought for completion as it seems timely and to be one of our most wicked problems to enable a society that works better for all of us.

# MARKET WITHOUT
# A NAME

Our future opportunities are the growing number of wicked problems. The Industrial Revolution created a market full of tame problems. New ways of working and production allowed us to create ever-evolving offers and in turn, these new capabilities have opened up wicked problems to be solved and offered on this new market. In other words, designing bespoke and hyper-personalized services used to be not viable. Today it is. The question is how to detect the wicked characteristics of those opportunities. A tame offer will not make you competitive in this market.

Does this mean you need a mobile app to be appealing? No! We need new descriptors and indicators to define the value in this new market. The level at which a service can be there for a customer, without the customer having to spend time and effort. The agility and flexibility of an offer to shift with context. The capability to enable a customer to solve a problem. These all go beyond selling a customer a product and then leaving them alone with it. That is not good enough anymore.

There is also a historical trend that can help us get a better sense of where things are going. In 1999, Joseph Pine wrote *The Experience Economy*, where he took the example of Starbucks to show how the service industry had evolved into an experience industry and how profit margins had evolved along with it. People were stunned when

Starbucks could charge $4 or more for a cup of coffee when brands like McDonald's had to stick around $2 per cup. The differentiator there was the emotional value of the "Italian" coffee experience of Starbucks. One cannot put a price on a feeling, yet Starbucks had just done that. Where McDonald's as a fast-food brand was stuck within the service-based market, Starbucks was one of the big players in the new experience market. Experiences were more complicated and more elaborate than the more transactional service market.

As in Alvin Toffler's *Future Shock*, the service market shocked the idea of a product-based market and businesses back in the 1960s and 1970s. Joseph Pine tracks these market phases back to a commodity phase between 1800 and 1900, a product phase until 1960 and the following service phase up until the start of the experience economy around 2000. If one follows that tendency, it means that market offers become more complex, but remain sustainable, because their profit margin grows exponentially. If the commodity market lasted one hundred years and the product market sixty years, the service market forty years and the experience market twenty years; then we might be right to assume a new market is already here. And maybe the challenge is to give this new market the name that describes its characteristics.

From a wicked and tame perspective, another trend can be mapped as long as an offer stays transactional: measuring the success of an offer and how an offer can be made by using quantitative measurements. This is where the experience economy made such a difference. You can't quantify an experience, because experience has an emotional component, and an offer is an experience. This has been the challenge for organizations and their communication departments for a while now. Everyone agrees on the impact of an emotional connection to a product, service or brand, but few have succeeded in creating one. It makes Apple fans queue up at 5 a.m. It makes advertising and branding agencies propose a "higher purpose" or "cause" approach for companies to try building an emotional connection with every customer. It surely indicates a step-change and much higher impact if you move from an offer that has a quantitative value to an offer that has a qualitative value. This is expressed in the Bain pyramid of values, which starts with transactional values at the bottom and ends with the highest emotional values at the top. The argument here is that companies that represent values from the top perform better. All this evidence points to qualitative value driving the future market. Tame companies that still make most of their decisions from tracking quantities will not be able to identify opportunities in this new market. Our new market has moved beyond just adding a qualitative value aspect.

The future market exists in a more complex and evolving space, one that has a qualitative rather than quantitative differentiator and can be bespoke on an individual level. If we take those abstract descriptors, I would say that the new market is a wicked problem-solving market. Leaving the abstraction level of product and service behind and moving beyond the addition of emotional value of an experience, the new offer would help solve existing problems more natural and more conveniently. Less interaction will be required but the benefits will be those of a lifehack or a behavioral nudge. People who didn't think they could save money will be able to. People who gave up their new year's gym membership will find better ways to stay fit. Communities will find better ways to engage around outcomes. All those are wicked problems, but we are finally in a position to solve some of them.

# Complexity
## does not make a
## Wicked Problem!

Knowing you are shooting
a moving target does.

# EPILOGUE

For a very long time, I have been looking at trends, tendencies, and viewpoints across industries and how they translated into the reality of many, many projects. The mainstream media likes to stick to the century-old narrative that times are changing faster than ever and that technology is the reason. Looking at my last twenty years of work and the books I read from the '50s, '60s, and '70s, I can't help but disagree. Times are changing, but our current pace only appears much faster because, for about a generation, progress in mindset, tools, and world were mostly ignored in favor of misleading narratives on what creates value. If you are looking at a world of wicked problems through tame eyes, it can be overwhelming. Without knowing, we have learned to expect wicked solutions in our lives as consumers, but have failed to understand this new world from the constraints of our tame companies. Consulting company Ernest & Young stipulates that the workplace is more critical to success than your education. Einstein commented that the only thing that interfered with his learning was education. Both quotes show the importance of context to mindset. You can design a better context in an organization that understands and solves problems differently.

People with wicked problem-solving skills will not flourish in a tame company. The commitment to support ideas needs to exist in every aspect of the company because every part needs to support it. Organizational or business agility does not just mean that things can be produced faster; it also means that ideas can be given more time and space to be explored and tried.

Agility is a significant step to becoming a bit more flexible by being more incremental. But too often I have seen it used as a speed funnel, not a quality and decision funnel. Agility is essentially a different way to segment your production process and sometimes your research and ideation process. It will only help you not to mess up on a large scale. The mess-ups will be on a small scale, and making them a learning process will benefit you. What agility does not do is create new thinking and new solutions. It is part of the "how," not the "why." I love agility, but I understand it is only a tool, and just like big data, prone to garbage-in, garbage-out. It can increase your efficiency and reduce the risk of each step but cannot improve your quality.

Design thinking is deconstructed by nature, just like agility is. I am pleased to see that some mental models that existed equally in engineering and design are finally coming together so that friction between the practices can be reduced. We still have a long way to go with tooling, but designers and coders are closer than ever to creating great things and more collaborative and transparent processes.

Managers need to disappear or shift their responsibility as decision-makers. Data and the capability to assess priority will come from many areas, and decisions need to be collaborative. A wicked problem will never be solved by a single specialist anymore, so why have a single decision maker?

What I am humbly trying to achieve with this book is a new way of looking at things. Shifting the narrative or improving a metaphor often brings understanding and reduces fear. I embraced this new mindset many years ago, and after I did, none of the shifts and changes of the last twenty years felt fast or overwhelming. To better understand the essence and underlying drivers of today and tomorrow will slow things down, make big complicated things look tame, and reveal the real problem ahead. Or so I hope.

The way we can solve problems has changed. Wicked problems are the new market. It is not just personalized mass production. We are not building faster horses. What is truly important is that none of this is rocket science. I have trained hundreds of people to create amazing new ideas, and it did not take them the twenty years it took me. I have yet to find any company or person I worked with who could not adopt a new way of working and looking at things. I have seen Jake Knapp teach five-day sprints in one day. I have been able to put dozens of teams on real projects within a few weeks. The only obstacles were silos, politics, specialist languages, or middlemen who were obsolete and knew it. These are not small obstacles, but they hold no power once you are aware of them.

Wicked and tame describe two different ways of problem-solving. I want to invite everyone to start calling it just that. I sometimes feel like how Tim Berners-Lee must feel when he wants everyone to reconsider a free flow of data. Our capitalist system has all the incentives to silo up processes, data, and other offerings. Every consultancy offers a different version of design thinking, agility, service design, et cetera, et cetera, et cetera. Please know that any of this can be freely downloaded on the *internet* and does not require large consultancies to give you a version of it in blue in exchange for half of your annual budget. Everyone "only cooks with water," as we say in Germany, meaning everyone is using the same recipe. Once we have established that, we should focus on the real challenge, which sits beyond tools and processes within the understanding of the problems ahead.

One of our biggest challenges is to bring the practices together and merge into a more flexible and accessible version of what exists today. Agility, design thinking, systems thinking, enterprise architecture, business analytics, business design, growth hacking, innovation, intrapreneurship . . . all of these professions and gatekeepers of tools need to be prepared to talk to each other.

The Stanford Life Design Lab[44] is living proof that some approaches can be transferred to any problem, even designing your own life. It uses human-centered design thinking to investigate and prototype your life opportunities. This is the kind of silo-busting we need today.

Technology will not give you an edge in the future; it has become too commoditized, a thing everyone has, just like everyone has electricity. Invest in the flexibility of people and ways of working that help you understand the world better. Listen to the insights that come back from research and from how teams are evolving the process. Solutions without problems kill organizations. Knowing the WHY will give you a market edge.

None of this is rocket science. I feel like I sound like someone from the '70s because the insights have been there for decades. As Esko Kilpi beautifully states, "Everything worth saying has been said before, but because not everyone was listening, I will repeat it in a slightly different manner."

I hope some of my words and examples will help you make better decisions and investments, bring different practices together, and let us all find a better way to do better things.

Exciting times ahead!

# TameProblems
## will get automated.

# Wicked Problems
## are the new marketplace.

# ABOUT THE AUTHOR

A Royal College of Art alumnus and ex-MIT Media Lab Europe researcher, Marcus Kirsch has worked as a transformation, service design, and innovation consultant and hands-on practitioner for over twenty years.

With project experience for companies like British Telecom, GlaxoSmithKline, Kraft, McDonald's, Nationwide, Nissan, Science Museum, P&G, Telekom Italia, and many others, he believes that we need a new narrative, mindset, and way of working to align ourselves with what society needs today.

When Marcus is not hard at work, he is a mediocre indoor climber, movie nerd, and maker. He currently resides in London, UK. *The Wicked Company* is Marcus's first book.

# BIBLIOGRAPHY

[1] Boiling Frog, fable, https://en.wikipedia.org/wiki/Boiling_frog

[2] Tame and Wicked Problems, https://www.open.edu/openlearn/ocw/mod/oucontent/view.php?id=65950&section=3.3

[3] MIT cross-disciplinary culture https://mitadmissions.org/apply/process/what-we-look-for/

[4] Wanderjahre (Journeyman years), https://en.wikipedia.org/wiki/Journeyman_years

[5] T-shaped skills, https://en.wikipedia.org/wiki/T-shaped_skills

[6] Robert Root-Bernstein, *Multiple Giftedness in Adults: The Case of Polymaths, https://link.springer.com/chapter/10.1007/978-1-4020-6162-2_42*

[7] Henry Ford, deskilling, https://en.wikipedia.org/wiki/Deskilling

[8] *The Zero Marginal Cost Society,* Jeremy Rifkin, https://www.amazon.co.uk/Zero-Marginal-Society-JEREMY-RIFKIN/dp/1137280115/

[9] Ken Robinson, TED Talk, Do schools kill creativity?, https://www.ted.com/talks/ken_robinson_says_schools_kill_creativity

[10] James Burke, Admiral Shovel and the toilet roll, https://archive.dconstruct.org/2012/admiralshovel

[11] Nilofer Merchant, The New How, https://www.amazon.co.uk/New-How-Paperback-Solutions-Collaborative/dp/1491903430/

[12] Esko Kilpi, Rethinking skills and responsibility, https://medium.com/@EskoKilpi/rethinking-skills-and-responsibility-78a0b76a859b

[13] Pine & Gilmore, The Experience Economy, https://www.amazon.co.uk/s?k=teh+experience+economy&ref=nb_sb_noss_2

[14] The Atlantic, Sean Parker influence on Facebook: https://www.theatlantic.com/technology/archive/2011/09/sean-parkers-greatest-creation-mark-zuckerberg/337662/

[15] Downsides of acronyms: https://www.mandel.com/blog/are-acronyms-hurting-or-helping-your-communications

[16] P&G acronyms : http://adage.com/article/special-report-pg-at-175/talking-internal-talk-p-g/237978/

[17] Tim O'Reilly, WTF?, https://www.amazon.co.uk/Wtf-Whats-Future-Why-Its/dp/0062699555/

[18] German Jewish Émigrés and US Invention, https://www.aeaweb.org/articles?id=10.1257/aer.104.10.3222

[19] Groningen in Deloitte Fast50, https://www.foundedingroningen.com/news/8-companies-from-groningen-in-the-deloitte-fast50

[20] Starbucks around the world, https://www.statista.com/statistics/266465/number-of-starbucks-stores-worldwide/

[21] Duncan J. Watts, Everything is Obvious, https://www.amazon.co.uk/gp/product/184887216X/

[22] Object-Oriented-Programming, https://en.wikipedia.org/wiki/Object-oriented_programming

[23] Package Switching, https://en.wikipedia.org/wiki/Packet_switching

[24] Bootlegs, https://en.wikipedia.org/wiki/Bootleg_recording

[25] PopcornTime, https://www.theverge.com/2015/9/10/9300083/popcorn-time-creator-sebastian-frederico-abad

[26] The Rise and Rise of Bitcoin, https://www.imdb.com/title/tt2821314/

[27] API stats, https://techcrunch.com/2016/05/21/the-rise-of-apis/

[28] David Epstein, Range, https://www.amazon.co.uk/Range-Generalists-Triumph-Specialized-World/dp/1509843493/

[29] Hal Valerian, Inexpensive communications, https://www.nytimes.com/2002/01/17/business/economic-scene-if-there-was-a-new-economy-why-wasn-t-there-a-new-economics.html

[30] Warren Bennis in Future Shocks, https://www.amazon.co.uk/ Future-Shock-Alvin-Toffler/dp/0808501526/

[31] Fortune, Value of Workers, http://fortune.com/2017/06/22/tech-automation-jobs/

[32] Gallup, Worker engagement poll, https://news.gallup.com/ poll/165269/worldwide-employees-engaged-work.aspx

[33] Michael Simmons, Polymaths, https://medium.com/the-mission/ modern-polymath-81f882ce52db

[34] Charles Murray, Human Accomplishments, https://www.amazon. com/Human-Accomplishment-Pursuit-Excellence-Sciences/ dp/006019247X/

[35] Scott Galloway, Do two things great, https://www.youtube.com/ watch?v=1T22QxTkPoM

[36] Carol Dweck, Growth Mindset, https://www.youtube.com/ watch?v=hiiEeMN7vbQ

[37] Harvard Business Review, Why you should have two careers, https://hbr.org/2017/04/why-you-should-have-at-least-two-careers

[38] Asymmetric Information and Entrepreneurship, https://papers. ssrn.com/sol3/papers.cfm?abstract_id=2596846

[39] Theory X and theory Y, https://www.mindtools.com/pages/ article/newLDR_74.htm

[40] Tom Kelley, The 12 faces of innovation, http://www.tenfacesofinnovation.com/

[41] Nicholas J. Carr, IT doesn't matter, https://hbr.org/2003/05/it-doesnt-matter

[42] L. David Marquet, Turn the Ship Around!, https://www.davidmarquet.com/turn-the-ship-around-a-true-story-of-turning-followers-into-leaders-by-david-marquet/

[43] Daniel Kahnemann, Thinking Fast and Slow, https://www.amazon.co.uk/Thinking-Fast-Slow-Daniel-Kahneman/dp/0141033576/

[44] Stanford Life Design Lab, http://lifedesignlab.stanford.edu/